PRODUCT PLANNING SIMPLIFIED

PRODUCT PLANNING SIMPLIFIED

Philip Marvin

 AMERICAN MANAGEMENT ASSOCIATION

© American Management Association, Inc., New York, 1972.
All rights reserved. Printed in the United States of America.

International standard book number: 0-8144-5299-X
Library of Congress catalog card number: 74-188844

First printing

To

Chester F. Carlson,
The Battelle Memorial Institute
and the Xerox Corporation

To those who exercised temerity and arrogance
in creating and producing a product
others said couldn't be made and couldn't be sold
—and wouldn't work, anyway.

Preface

THE first thing that strikes one about corporation growth—either as an investor or as a business manager—is that some management groups seem to know how to expand their scale of operation while others don't. Small companies surpass older, established ones. Larger corporations surpass their contemporaries.

Size, then, isn't the crucial factor in achieving growth goals—it's know-how. To prepare to appraise a company's growth prospects, one can talk with top executive groups in various companies representing various industries and compare growth companies with companies that aren't growing. From this, one learns that it's important to ask four searching questions.

First, does management understand the concepts and operating fundamentals basic to establishing the targets, timetables, and techniques that lead to growth? Some grasp these, others don't. Again, it isn't a matter of company size or age. Both small and large companies have expanded and are expanding, while others are not. Both well-established and recently organized management teams have been successful in growth planning. Others have failed miserably.

Revitalizing management thinking within an organization isn't easy. The situation is a sensitive one. If concepts are introduced before the way has been prepared for them, management cannot assimilate them. Progress is sacrificed. Leadership must come from the top—and programs must be implemented at the next level by managers who know the ins and outs of what's involved in planning for growth. One of the greatest stumbling blocks has been to succumb to some current management fad as a panacea.

Second, is the future being planned? In observing the operations of a number of companies at close range, and critically, it's possible to establish what differentiates corporate growth from corporate stagnation. When one spends time with members of the management team in successful companies, one finds significantly similar patterns of action. The same is true in less successful operations.

Managers of the latter have often become so preoccupied with today's business that they forget all about tomorrow's business. Thus stagnation occurs, both in some of the older corporations and in some of the newer, currently expanding ones.

Not only is it important to examine management practices in growth companies, but this examination must be made at critical points in order to find out what has proved valuable in implementing programs. This can be learned only from those who actually did the job. The mere fact that management wants to expand operations isn't enough. Men must be available who know how to go about doing this. Growth companies have these men. It's what they're doing that's important.

Third, what technology is needed? Future business will depend on the ability of managers to manage technology. Therefore, what technology is needed—

To insure that the corporation will continue to operate in areas of growing business activity and profit potential?

To make the best possible use of corporation resources such as raw materials, technical specialties, and management talent?

To utilize available markets adequately?

To insure steadily increasing and stable profits?

To contribute to the corporation's ability to accept social and humanitarian responsibilities?

Fourth, can the use of this technology be accelerated without incurring excessive costs? There has been a tendency on the part of some to develop a successful solution to a problem and then stick with it long after it has served its purpose. This practice won't lead to profits from technology—because of technology's dynamic aspects. Yesterday's practices must yield to new answers.

An advertisement for the Stearns automobile at the beginning of this century made an amazing claim: "Use it until it wears out. There will never be a car materially better, for invention in this line has about reached the limit—to build anything better, with man's present knowledge, is utterly out of the question."

One doesn't hear much today about the Stearns automobile or

companies that were sure of having all the answers. Others, however, who were sure they didn't have all the answers are among the present industrial giants. Technology was growing, and they grew with it. Today, technology is growing at such a rate that it calls for sweeping reappraisals of traditional thinking if management is to more effectively turn it into profits.

The very rapidity with which scientific breakthroughs are taking place creates special hazards for business managers. Specifically the danger is this—preoccupation with the glamour of discovery tends to make people forgetful of the need to adjust to new demands arising from changing technology.

A few create problems for all. If no one were concerned, the problem wouldn't be acute—but such isn't the case. Some are learning to run with new ideas while others are learning to walk. The resulting inequality in the distribution of rewards is noticeable.

The chief executive of a company that ranks high in the growth category of American business remarked that his company had been concentrating on reducing the time it takes to turn a new idea into profit-producing hardware. He pointed to a familiar but hidden cost of ideas in the development phase. Aside from development costs themselves, each day in development represents a day of lost sales dollars—a day of lost returns on invested capital. This is of course obvious, but it's not always easy for some to see the obvious.

Focusing top management thinking on the obvious, this executive has developed a way to shorten the idea-to-profit interval by better than 30 percent. Prospects for shortening this time interval even more look good.

A company's growth curve is merely an envelope reflecting the performance of the individual products that make up the product portfolio of the business. Most businesses get their start from a single good idea, quite frequently from an idea that went begging for attention. Someone or some few sensed its potential and started a business venture to capitalize on an idea others had turned down. Business after business can trace its origin to courageous innovation.

Once this process of courageous innovation is over, however, something seems to happen. The business pioneer turns his coonskin and buckskins in for a dark fedora and a gray flannel suit. The pioneer turns conservative. He becomes allergic to "newness." He rejects the very process of innovation that gave him his start in business life. He may do a good job with what he has in hand, but he's out of the race to capitalize on new opportunities. He leaves future innovation to the more vigorous and courageous.

It's equally dangerous to swing to the opposite extreme. The secret of success isn't necessarily "firstness." While most businesses can trace their start to a single good product idea, it doesn't always follow that it's best to be first every time. Sound judgment is essential in transforming new technology into profit-producing products.

Picking and choosing new products isn't easy. To be really interesting to those skilled in guiding growth programs, a product proposal must satisfy certain criteria that have proved useful in evaluating product ideas. The new product must be

1. One that fits logically into the company's existing lines of business or is compatible with management's projected thinking.
2. One for which there is an anticipated market demand.
3. One for which raw materials can be made available.
4. One that can be manufactured and sold profitably over at least a normal payout.
5. One that can be produced with existing plant facilities or, where new facilities are required, one where the capital investment and resulting depreciation charges are not excessive in relation to the volume of business and selling price that can be anticipated.
6. One for which the company possesses the manpower and facilities to develop, manufacture, and introduce.
7. One for which the development and introduction costs can be amortized in at least a normal payout.
8. One upon which the return on investment can be estimated with reasonable accuracy.
9. One that the company is financially in a position to develop and introduce.

In any product venture a company may be an innovator, a leader, a follower, or a laggard. The important thing is to be able to choose the proper category for the right reasons at the proper time rather than to fall into the same category every time through force of habit.

Those who have been successful in achieving growth have put themselves in a position where they could pick and choose their way, drawing on the full resources of the corporation. Those who have been able to pick and choose have been able to capitalize on three fundamental growth factors.

First, management groups in successful growth businesses have learned how to develop data for decision making. In the long run, time is saved and decisions are easier to make if the necessary background information is developed first. The alternative course usually

involves a greater amount of time and energy in corrective measures
to repair damages resulting from hasty decisions.

Some commit themselves to decisions too soon—before they are
compelled to act. These executives subscribe to the "strike directly
at the problem" school. This is in theory good, but is rarely practical
because most of the time it's not possible to focus directly on the
problem. Others, among them the more successful decision makers,
take a more leisurely approach. They gather relevant facts and feel
their way toward a solution.

Second, growth companies get more mileage out of their resources.
For example, if today's supply of manpower were effectively utilized,
there wouldn't be any talk of shortages in selected areas. A surplus
of time would be available to achieve goals now considered by some
to be out of reach.

Third, successful management groups have learned to make effective use of their technical output. One of the greatest wastes of a
corporation's time, money, and manpower today shows up in research,
engineering, and new-product-development activities. Why? Because
the corporation isn't structured to absorb and use new knowledge
and new products as rapidly as they are created.

On one familiar pretext or another, good ideas are shelved while
management orients itself to the newness of ideas. But where competitors are able to move faster, markets are lost.

Those who have produced outstanding growth records have been
successful in capitalizing on these fundamental growth factors. They
do a better overall job of decision making. They make better use
of their resources. They make better-than-average use of the output
of creative thinking.

It's going to be more important for management to capitalize on
these growth factors in the future than it has been in the past. These
factors have been important growth determinants in the past, but
in the days ahead they will be even more important as determinants
of continued corporate existence.

The current competitive climate presents some problem areas of
unusual significance. These complicate the picture for those who like
to proceed in an orderly, unhurried, and undisturbed manner. At
the same time they create opportunities for those companies structured to capitalize on them.

First, technology is a dynamic force. It's the arch foe of established
order and procedure. It creates constantly changing conditions. It
creates radically new opportunities. Each must be examined in its
own setting, not as something to be adapted to present ways of doing

business but as an opportunity to be capitalized on by management methods tailored to new needs. Up-to-the-minute orientation, information, motivation, techniques, and skills are essential if managers are to turn new technology into profits.

Second, the management of scientists, engineers, inventors, planners, application specialists, and others who turn ideas into salable hardware calls for special talents. The most important is balance. Men who can sense the potential in new ideas without forgetting the needs of the present are the men for the job. No new idea is worth anything to a business if its impact will be disastrously disruptive to the company's bread-and-butter resources. But anything new is disturbing to a degree.

Such men are available. They have been indispensable to growth in the past. They will be indispensable to future growth and achievement. They are neither hapless visionaries nor conformists clinging to past practices. They can sense future opportunities and appraise real values gained in the past. Their knowledge, judgment, experience, and innate ability lead to decision-making balance.

Only such managers can effectively guide new programs. Too many abortive attempts by self-styled experts have failed because of a lack of a real "feel" for the tools of the trade.

Third, investment in technology, soundly administered, not only has proved to pay its way but to yield dividends that can be reinvested in greatly expanded new programs. This aspect is an asset to those who had the foresight to start early programs. To all others, it's an insidious threat. Those who are behind can't catch up easily. Even if they could set up a soundly organized program, they would still have to cope with a built-in time lag of serious magnitude.

Firms spend money on technology because they have found that they can increase their earnings at an above-average rate through the development of new technology. Earlier research pays the cost of the research that follows. There's a multiplier effect. Yesterday's new products provide today's profits.

Fourth, the gap between manufacturing output and capacity creates problems too. These must also be resolved by technological development.

The climate in which business operates creates very real opportunities. Some will capitalize on them, others will neglect them. The big achievements will depend primarily on technological capabilities, but not on just spending more money. Indeed, the expenditure of less money may yield greater returns—when this money is spent effectively.

It's time to toughen up management thinking about technology, to think in depth as well as breadth, to think in terms of the full scope of possible activities, and to hold technology responsible for figuring out what will pay off and when. This responsibility can't be shifted to others. As one keen-minded thinker once observed:

> There is still much to do—even if it turns out that the ancients discovered everything, the application, the perception of cause and effect, and further development of that which has been discovered by others will always remain new.

Seneca made that statement more than 1,900 years ago. There is, indeed, still much to do.

Philip Marvin

prologue
Planning Ahead

To search out and apply new knowledge of phenomena, materials, and the arts that can be used by the corporation.

To identify problems that must be solved with regard to functions, materials, and applications.

To create products, processes, and services customers will want; that can be produced, distributed, installed, maintained, and serviced, at prices customers will pay.

To make the best possible use of the corporation's resources such as raw materials, technical specialities, and management talent.

To insure that the corporation will continue to operate in areas of growing business activity and profit potential.

To yield returns on the corporation's investment greater than those offered by alternative uses of the corporation's capital.

To put the corporation and its customers in the best possible position with respect to defined goals.

To contribute to the corporation's ability to accept social and humanitarian responsibilities.

Contents

1 A Précis for Policy Makers   1

Part One   Finding and Screening

2 Ten Key Factors in Successful Product Development   15
3 Developing Ideas for New Products   23
4 Picking Profitable Products   32
5 Pricing New Products   44
6 Projecting the Profitability of New Products   51

Part Two   Funding and Auditing

7 Funding Product Development   65
8 Profit Opportunities in Present Products   72
9 The Protectable Part of Proprietary Product and
      Process Positions   82
10 Auditing Product Programs   91
11 Why New Products Fail   104
12 Checkpoints in New Product Pioneering   117
13 Sharpening Up Decision Making   124

Part Three   Organizing

14 Detecting and Defining Potentially Profitable Technology   135
15 Integrating Technology and Markets   150
16 Research for Results   161
17 Fundamentals of Engineering Organization   174
18 Evaluating Engineering Operations   190

Part Four   Staffing

19   The New Product Manager: Filter or Innovator?   203
20   Developing Creative Capabilities   209

Index   215

1

A Précis
for Policy Makers

AS in the past, industry leaders of the future will be those who have noted corporate needs and learned to meet them immediately. Keeping up with the Joneses isn't enough in business operations, when being first can be an asset. Real leaders don't deal in averages. They set averages for others to achieve. Their acute awareness aids them in developing a sensitivity to situations and details. They detect ways and means of turning opportunities into profits.

There aren't any secrets of success in the sense that they are inscribed on a parchment and safely secured in the inner recesses of a vault owned by one of the more prosperous companies. Most successful executives will admit that many of the keys to prosperity for their companies would only have unlocked doors to disaster in other businesses. The important thing to determine, these men add, is what's good for your own company.

But one suspects that there are certain clues or guidelines having more or less universal applicability that would help management profit from the experience of others in planning for growth. These guidelines may be found by analyzing the individual experience of executives and looking for the reasons behind success or failure. Some clues to growth and success have been repeatedly emphasized.

Such clues don't disclose new managerial concepts or radically different techniques. Rather, they reveal some common shortcomings that have cropped up when management's time and attention have been diverted by a myriad of other matters. In that they reveal serious pitfalls, they might justifiably be called secrets of success in planning for growth. Five specific questions provide keys to these clues:

1. Are the basic ingredients of growth recognized?
2. Are profit-producing responsibilities clearly positioned?
3. Are performance-measurement areas known and understood?
4. How does the product plan fit into the risk spectrum?
5. Is size growing faster than earnings?

Are the Basic Ingredients of Growth Recognized?

Before planning ahead for growth, it is important to have a clear concept of the factors that contribute to business growth. Companies that have developed in size, strength, and income have capitalized on four opportunities for growth. These are (1) growth markets, (2) capital accumulation, (3) technical advances, and (4) creative merchandising.

The first calls attention to opportunities created by a population increase, bringing with it as it does, the need for more products. Capital accumulation gives a business a resource to work with and the opportunity to multiply management's effectiveness as a profit producer. Technological advances reveal new directions for product and process exploitation. Creative merchandising provides the opportunity of acquiring a greater share of customer dollars. All of these must be combined with the ability to turn opportunities into a profitable return on the investment involved.

Are Profit-producing Responsibilities Clearly Positioned?

An important ingredient of success is the fixing of profit-producing responsibilities. The effectiveness of the overall profit picture in a going business is considerably enhanced if responsibility for it can be delegated to individuals who will have the authority to take effective action in discharging it.

The responsibility and authority for decision making must be placed at the action point, where opportunities and problems can be identified and comprehended and where men can turn on a dime when necessary to do what must be done. In addition, men who can act effectively must be developed. Responsibilities must be such that they do not require unique abilities and indispensable men to carry them out, because indispensable men create problems in any organization.

In fixing profit-producing responsibilities, decision-making authority to be most effective should fall into clearly discernible performance areas that, taken in toto, create the return on investment that characterizes managerial leadership in growth corporations.

Are Performance-measurement Areas Known and Understood?

In any operation, eight performance measurement areas are important.

1. Profitability	2. Productivity
3. Position	4. Products
5. Planning	6. Personnel
7. Policies	8. Progress

Each of these eight performance-measurement areas could well be the subject of detailed scrutiny. In any business, self-examination should be a continuing practice. Performance measurement is the basis of business health and growth. The eight performance areas provide focal points that facilitate measurement.

Certain of these eight performance-measurement areas assume a disproportionate magnitude. This doesn't impair the usefulness of the others as performance-measurement guides. Their primary purpose is to aid in the evaluation of the effectiveness of operations. Privately owned businesses exist to produce a profit on invested capital by selling a product. That product may be a tangible commodity or an intangible service. Whichever it is, or both, the product is the basis of a growing business. In the course of time, a single product grows into multiple products and product lines. These "product centers" provide a point of application for performance measurement.

1. *Profitability.* The profitability of a product center is one of the first measurements to be made in evaluating total performance. Judgment must be exercised in striking a balance between current profit producers and potential profit producers. One is as important as the other to the success of a business. In the long view, runners-up may be as important as today's winners in the product scene.

Special attention should be called to one facet of the measurement of profit performance. Products fall below breakeven points in their declining days, points they passed on their way up when the product enjoyed its growth phase. When a product passes the breakeven point on its way up it's noticed, but the significance of the breakeven point of a product with declining sales is often overlooked.

Products with records of declining sales place demands on management time and corporation resources just as much as products having better long-term outlooks. Unless someone takes cognizance of this fact and then takes action to eliminate these poor performers, profitability will suffer.

Profitability as a performance measurement calls for a three-sided, or stereo, concept encompassing (1) height of profit levels, (2) breadth of base, and (3) profit trend—upward or downward.

2. *Productivity.* Every function the business performs in the course of its operations associated with each product's profit-producing center should be subjected to an analysis to determine the degree to which it approaches maximum effectiveness. This is the only way of determining how close actual income is to reaching upper limits of potentially procurable levels.

A common error that leads to loss through unrealized income results from the acceptance of certain profit levels as satisfactory without having any basis for the assumption that these levels are the best that can be achieved. Measurement of the productivity of each function forms the only basis for establishing criteria of acceptability. Hidden opportunities leading to greater profits have been revealed by taking a new look at operations to measure productivity on an across-the-board functional basis. The productiveness of the research, engineering, manufacturing, and selling functions should be evaluated in this process.

Two questions are important in examining each operation from the product-idea-development stage to the ultimate dollar-profit stage: (1) Are we doing this job as well as it can be done? (2) How sure are we of the accuracy of our measurement of the relative productivity of this operation?

Productivity measurement is more than a detailed analytical process. It has diagnostic and therapeutic overtones as well. In establishing performance criteria, new standards of performance and improved operating procedures are inevitably developed or acquired. These byproducts represent money in the bank in a very real sense.

Productivity as a performance measurement has two dimensions— quantity and quality. Depending on the demands of the particular situation, one must give some ground to the other. Determining how much ground to give might be considered to add a third dimension.

3. *Position.* The product's industry position is an important measurement of performance. Each product should be rated against its competitors with respect to significant factors, including sales volume, market coverage and penetration, style, design, consumer acceptance, price, and manufacturing cost.

The results of such measurements are useful in developing strengths and discovering weaknesses in each product center. Such data should not be regarded as absolute. If it is found, for example, that sales of a particular product surpass those of others in the industry, this fact by itself does not prove that market opportunities are exhausted. Only by a study of market potential can this conclusion be reached.

A product's relative position with reference to each factor measured serves to highlight areas where the need for further analysis and action is indicated. Analysis is needed in order to compare industry position with optimums that could be obtained through more productive operations. Action is needed to achieve these optimums. Measurement of performance in the industry will in many cases provide a clue to the priority and sense of urgency that should attach to specific programs to be undertaken in developing added strength in each product center as a base for future profits.

4. *Products.* Measurement of performance in the product center should determine the degree to which products meet the test of design for consumer acceptance, satisfactory performance, economical production, distribution depth and breadth, effective merchandising, ease of installation, adequate servicing, and ultimate replacement.

Beyond these considerations, products should be examined with respect to the establishment and achievement of sound product objectives. Each product should be positioned with respect to its own individual life cycle and the basic objectives of the product offerings of the business. The composite picture reveals the degree to which the company is meeting these objectives and protecting its future earnings by assuring a continuing supply of new products to replace those becoming obsolete as products pass through the ten distinct periods constituting a product life cycle. These are the prospective, speculative, potentially profitable, scheduled, development, introduction, growth, competitive, obsolescence, and dropout periods.

The composite picture also tells whether or not the company is taking full advantage of every opportunity to introduce lower cost products, restyled items, and products designed for improved performance. It also reveals what the company is doing about new markets and new uses.

5. *Planning.* Effective planning determines to a large degree the profitability of each product center. It can take so long for products to be passed on to the consumer that the initial plans will have been forgotten. Yet to these first plans, as much as to subsequent ones, should accrue credits for success and debits for failure.

One of the significant measures of performance is that of the effectiveness of the planning process. Product planning calls for programs encompassing research and engineering, resource development, commercial development, plant and equipment development, staff development, and return on capital investment.

Plans should meet three important needs. They should state targets to be achieved. They should provide timetables for the achievement of especially important targets. They should detail techniques for reaching the desired end results. These three criteria of targets, timetables, and techniques provide the basis for measuring planning effectiveness.

6. *Personnel.* The degree to which manpower has been developed is another important measure of overall performance. Measurement of performance in this area should be both broad and deep. The background and interests of the directors of the corporation should be considered one of the elements of this evaluation. These men have the last word in determining the destiny of all programs.

At the policy and operating level, the interests, background and experience of those identified with individual product centers should be subjected to careful analysis. Beyond this it is necessary to know the availability of the specialized talent and skill required to put new programs into motion and to carry out and achieve the objectives of current programs.

In measuring manpower performance five aspects are important. They are (1) the ability of the individual to perform his presently assigned function, (2) his ability to accept increased responsibility, (3) the specific action he takes to prepare for increased responsibility, (4) the degree to which the individual subordinates his personal interests to the job at hand, (5) his ability to inspire associates to higher levels of performance.

7. *Policies.* Policies are governing guides to action that enable managers to exercise initiative and at the same time operate within established organizational concepts as conceived by top level management. When men must make decisions they must know not only the limits to their authority, they must know the general rules of action to which top management wants them to adhere. Policies make top

management thinking known. These policies guide action into compatible channels for effective overall operations.

Each product center should be studied to determine what policies are applicable, their adequacy to cover specific needs, their relationship to the needs of other product centers, the degree to which policies are generally known, their clarity of expression, and their stability over a period of time. These and other pertinent aspects should be evaluated.

The formulation and statement of policies is a top management responsibility. The measurement of performance is made at the product center. This is where the full impact of policy making is felt. The effectiveness of decisions and the effort required in making them are directly related to the availability of sound policy guides.

8. *Progress.* The final performance-measurement area directs attention to the evaluation of the progress made in each product center. In making this measurement, the important question to be answered is: To what degree have growth opportunities been capitalized?

Performance should be measured against what could have been achieved if every available opportunity had been exhausted. The question above breaks down into two questions: How much progress has been made? How much progress could have been made? In making this measurement, it isn't of any particular consequence to know what competitors have accomplished unless such information serves as a partial indication of levels of potential achievement. The real test is what could have been accomplished by high-level talent supplied with adequate resources within the given period of time.

The eight performance-measurement areas and the results of these evaluations focus attention on degrees of relative achievement in each area. Performance is measured against top levels of potential achievement. Product centers are chosen as the basis for measurement. These product centers are profit centers as well and performance at these centers is a matter of major management concern.

Performance measurements shouldn't be regarded as ultimate ratings of activities in product centers or in overall performance. These measurements are simply guides. There are many occasions when compromises must be made. Give and take comes into play in all business activities. To improve performance in one area, sacrifices are called for in others. At the same time it's important to make measurements periodically to determine the magnitude of the advances or setbacks in each of the eight areas in order to relate causes, effects, and associated profits and losses as they occur. The knowledge gained by this is valuable in future decision making.

How Does the Product Plan Fit into the Risk Spectrum?

Risk is an inherent ingredient in business operations. Notwithstanding the general acceptance of this fact, business risks and particularly those associated with product planning aren't always viewed in their full perspective.

Product risks can be arrayed in a spectrum ranging from a general category of readily acceptable products sold in reasonably well defined and developed markets at one extreme to radically different products that must pioneer new markets at the other extreme. Risk must be incorporated in planning.

Profits are often associated with risk taking and not unreasonably so, but it would be a mistake to assume that high profits and high risk are inseparable. Rather, from a product-planning position there are opportunities for both speculative and calculable profits. Speculative profits call for a high degree of imaginative ability and pioneering spirit. There is little basis for projecting experience. Calculable profits are based on the adequacy and availability of historical data as a basis for projections into the future.

Any undertaking brings into play opportunities for both speculative and calculable profits. Executives charged with product responsibilities should evaluate these, using the risk-spectrum concept as a tool.

A product's position in the risk spectrum calls for a reexamination of three significant factors: (1) appraisal of relative risk, (2) acceptability of risk, and (3) access to funds. These three aspects of risks associated with product planning are inseparable. Management must know, as can best be determined, how much risk is involved in a particular undertaking in order to arrive at a conclusion as to whether or not it is an acceptable level of risk in the light of the funds that will be required by the program.

Positioning products in the risk spectrum is an important undertaking. Risks should be reduced to quantitative terms in the best way possible.

Is Size Growing Faster Than Earnings?

Size can be a liability as well as an asset. Bigness can be hazardous unless the added resources it brings with it can be utilized effectively to offset the dangers inherent in size. It is part of the American dream to want to be big. Product planners should think big—but they should examine the problems associated with growth to make certain that programs capitalize on size and turn it from a millstone into a mile-stone. If size turns out to be truly a millstone the business will sink—as have so many successful smaller businesses when they have crossed the threshold into big business. In sharp contrast, those who have recognized the problems as well as the advantages have prospered.

Where growth has more to do with size than profit, the reasons for it are commonly revealed by answers to four questions. They have proved useful in probing into this troublesome syndrome.

First, is product addition matched by product deletion? Both are important. New products maintain the vitality of product centers through lowered cost, better styling, improved performance, additional markets, and new uses. Any one or any combination of these factors is important in developing and expanding product centers. But it is equally important to make certain that products are dropped from the portfolio when they cease to be profit producers.

Developing new products requires both imagination and initiative. So does dropping products that have become obsolete. Of the two functions, product deletion is the more neglected. After all, it's difficult to drop almost any product from the line. As long as sales volume exists it's only human to follow the easiest course of action and let things coast along. Add to this the fact that when products are dropped there are always a few customers for such items who are vociferous in their objections. These are just two of the reasons why product deletion is neglected.

Every product in the portfolio exhausts a portion of the company's resources by placing demands on funds, managerial time, technical staffs, facilities, and other resources. Profits result from striking the best possible balance between value paid and value received in using these resources. Many times specific products place greater demands on the company's resources than are returned on the basis of comparison with returns from some alternative product programs. The fact that a product produces a profit is not enough; the test is whether the product produces a greater profit than could be gained by using resources in another way.

When profit positions don't keep pace with growth, it's time to check on the number of products that have been dropped from the line as well as the number that have been added. Carrying products beyond the period when the rate of return falls behind the return from alternative programs is a major cause of slippage in profit position.

Second, do high profits hide high costs? Growth and prosperity make managers complacent. When this happens, costs rise disproportionately. One of the focal points of excessive costs is hidden in high-profit lines. When profits are high almost everyone seems to feel that it is no longer necessary to be cost-conscious. This, of course, is a sheer absurdity. The only justification for any element of cost lies in its ability to improve the profit position. When profits are high, costs should be scrutinized even more carefully than when profits are not high, because more money is involved.

The gamble may be great in attempting to improve the profit position of product lines in the high-profit category by incurring new costs. Cost increments too often exceed profit increments. One of the real opportunities for effective cost-reduction programs centers on high-profit lines.

Third, do profit leaders get as much attention as loss leaders? This amplifies the preceding question. Product lines operating in the red attract attention immediately. Those lines operating at a profit aren't examined as closely. Yet the real losses from operating profit leaders at levels below maximum efficiency may be greater than the total losses from all the lines that are operating in the red because of the high dollar volume inherent in established and profitable product lines.

No one wants losses. It's obviously bad business to have red figures on the books, but the really important point is to have the total profit at the highest possible level. The best way to accomplish this may be to direct attention to lost efficiency in high-profit lines first and to look at low-volume loss leaders last.

Generally, profit leaders are high-dollar-volume lines. When this is true, small economies, simply on a percentage basis, exert a tremendous impact on the profit position.

To go beyond operating economies, it should be pointed out that time spent on loss leaders shouldn't be at the expense of a failure to capitalize on the full potential of profit producers. These proven performers should be given every opportunity to exploit their full usefulness as contributors to the company's profits. They should have first call on every resource available. In these profit centers, every phase of the product's life cycle and every function from planning through production to promotion should receive the attention needed to take full advantage of a product's capacity to produce profits. Time and resources directed to the further development of profit producers can be substantially more productive than time spent troubleshooting in behalf of loss leaders.

Again, it should be emphasized that this should not be construed to suggest that loss leaders should be neglected. The important point to keep in mind is the fact that resources—administrative, technical, and operating, as well as capital—should be deployed in a way to produce the greatest profits. Too often, profits are sacrificed in putting out brush fires in a forest of loss leaders.

Fourth, are responsibilities for troubleshooting and problem-solving jobs shifted to consultants? When profits fail to keep pace with growth, it may mean that administrative talents are spread too thin. Well-managed companies grow in size. This is inevitable. As growth takes place, the management team must grow as well. If the technical and administrative group that initiates growth doesn't expand, too, progress is stifled and profits suffer.

One of the symptoms indicating that management development isn't keeping pace with growth is employment of outside consultants. Consultants can serve a useful purpose in providing extra legs and arms in special situations that arise from time to time. But the need for such extra help should be studied carefully to make sure that it will be nonrecurring and that it grows out of a special situation that doesn't reflect on the ability of the management team in technical and nontechnical areas. If a consultant is hired to do a job because the present management didn't act soon enough or adequately, the management team is failing to grow as expanded operations require.

At best no group assembled by a consulting firm from available staff members can ever approach the effectiveness of well-integrated company management. First, there is the risk that the staff assigned to the job by the consultant has been drawn from the on-the-shelf staff rather than the best-qualified members, who may already be working on other jobs. Then, too, the consultant must develop a familiarity with the company situation before he can even start work. None of this necessarily reflects on the desire or willingness of most consultants to do the best possible job. After all, consultants are in business to sell a commodity and this commodity, staff time, must be productive if the consultant is to stay in business. Consulting staffs put in long hours, at the customer's expense, in an effort to overcome these obstacles in performing the job they have been hired to do. The fact that they can't operate at higher levels of effectiveness is not usually attributable to lack of effort—but profits to the company are measures of results, not efforts.

To maintain profit growth, managerial resources must expand as operations grow. The use of consultants for troubleshooting and problem solving should be examined closely because their employment may be an early indication of the failure of the management team to expand with business growth.

part one
Finding and Screening

2

Ten Key Factors
in Successful
Product Development

ONE executive sums up his company's product expansion thinking in words to this effect:

"Our job is to gain supremacy over competitors by doing a better job in a shorter time in bringing out new products. These products must offer new function, better performance, or lower cost. Each of these values is readily marketable.

"Our business just won't stand still. Either it will grow or shrink. We plan to have it grow. The job won't be easy, but we're going to tackle it. If we can't take it, we want to know why."

This is a clear-cut expression of the competitive picture and the role new products play in achieving superiority. Unfortunately, however, product development programs frequently fall far short of anticipated goals. The manpower and ammunition of these programs are costly if not offset by profitable results in the form of tangible products. Analysis reveals ten key factors in successful product development.

Take Time for Development

Product development takes time. Many manufacturers are preoccupied with their going products. This means that development projects must be put off, often until too late. Business mortality figures attest to this fact.

Stagnation is the penalty for neglecting business development. Not too long ago the chief executive of a medium-size corporation remarked that business development was one of his major concerns because his firm hadn't accomplished anything new in the past ten years. There had been a lot of talk but no action. It didn't take much exploration to discover that everyone in the organization was too busy with day-to-day jobs.

Being too busy with today's job offers competitors the best possible opportunity to capture the market with new and improved lines.

Know the Steps

Product programs that take into account changes in consumer demands, new product developments by competitors, and many other pertinent factors require a thorough understanding of each step in the course of development. To insure successful product development programs, it is important to make certain that those who are assigned to this important job have such an understanding.

Every product sold today started somewhere as an idea. Successful products represent ideas that have been developed through a sequence of logically ordered steps designed to lead to marketable products. One of the major pitfalls in product programs results from not knowing these steps.

Here are three cases in point. The first, a machine-tool builder, neglected to inquire about the use of new metals in a particular industry while designing and developing a single-purpose machine that proved to be virtually worthless because of a subsequent change in material specifications in the part processed. The change could have been easily anticipated. The second, a manufacturer, was forced to undertake extensive redesign of a new product because building codes and electrical codes had not been duly considered. The third, also a manufacturer, was unable to sell an item because the color of the product failed to have competitive eye appeal.

In each of these instances an essential step in product development was omitted.

Join Knowledge with Ability

Specialized talent is a prerequisite to success in product development. Men in responsible positions must have the right mixture of abilities. Regardless of the way the group is brought together—from entirely inside the organization, from partly inside and partly outside the organization, or as a wholly outside group—one thing should be certain—all of the required talents must be represented on the team.

Few companies can expect to find within their organization all of the kinds of specialized help needed for the development of new products. Moreover, few firms will find that they can profitably use on a full-time basis the varied array of talent needed for the job at hand. But, whatever the circumstances, specialists must be made available when needed or the product development project will suffer. In the long run this means lost dollars in sales. No adequate substitute exists for specialized talent. Vacancies are more expensive than the personnel required to fill them.

As technology advances, competitive requirements change. Some talent is no longer required and new needs arise that must be satisfied to maintain a competitive product development program.

Frequent examples of deficiencies in this direction are encountered in the heavy equipment industry. Design often becomes merely a matter of making minor detailed changes in drawings. These drawings may be 25 years old or older. Forging ahead like a team of snails, such companies are quicky engulfed by more progressive companies whose capable staffs are applying modern stress-analysis techniques, advanced metallurgical and fabrication practices, new alloys, and newly developed design principles, and incorporating the latest techniques in instrumentation and control in new products.

The ability to apply new knowledge is just as important as knowing that it should be applied and is essential to productivity. Knowledge must be joined with the ability to apply this knowledge when new products are developed.

Draw on Experience

Product development assignments executed by competent and experienced personnel move swiftly and surely toward desired objectives. Experience lends efficiency. Where experience is not available, the staff must be supplemented to provide this important ingredient.

As the old expression has it: "Don't send a boy to do a man's job." Both may know how to cut wood, but the man's added efficiency will usually more than offset the lower hourly cost of the boy's labor.

Without any reflection on the ability of the recent graduate, his efficiency will be low until he has acquired skill through practice.

He will be a better man ten years later if he has had the wise counsel and guidance of experienced men.

One aircraft executive has had bitter experience with inexperienced but otherwise capable personnel assigned to a product development program. The men on the job were too green. They had the time, they knew the steps and had ability, but they lacked practice. As a consequence, their efficiency was unsatisfactory. Hard work was not enough to halt the corporation's slide. The new men couldn't move fast enough to keep ahead in a rapidly advancing aircraft industry. The job called for experienced men.

"What's wrong?" may well be asked if these men had the time, knew the steps, and had the ability. Simply this—too much time was being used to learn the way around and to develop the skill that must come from practice in any profession. This process takes time.

Practice is the bedrock of performance. Ability alone is not enough. Product programs need men who have acquired the experience that enables them to move with assurance and dispatch.

Develop Planning Techniques

Techniques are tools in product programming. Techniques are tested systems of organized attack on problems. They make possible efficient application of experience and ability in problem solving.

Good techniques for approaching problem areas are usually developed by those who have sufficient repetitive volume of product development work. Practice permits development of efficient and systematic ways of solving problems. Sound techniques develop from the repeated application of ability and experience.

Techniques for approaching product problems vary both in degree and in kind. Highly developed systems of product programming are generally found where results have been outstanding. Systems range from simple checklists to volumes of procedural data covering every major department in the organization.

The executive committee of one corporation schedules weekly meetings in which the product development director reports on new product ideas and studies. This report is based on a carefully established procedure for systematically searching for and screening new ideas. Current and comprehensive reporting is made possible by techniques for quickly appraising ideas, including both the technical and market aspects.

A pioneer products department has been established in this corporation. Here new product ideas get immediate attention. These techniques have been developed to provide the best possible method of expediting a steady flow of new products into the channels of production and selling.

View Problems in Perspective

For some years one equipment-parts manufacturer has been attempting to develop a consumer item to sell under a proprietary name. Attempts have been unsuccessful. The principal reason for failure has been that, because of the inherent nature of the business, the consumer-item concept is foreign to customary thinking.

As a parts manufacturer, the company is spoon-fed orders for specific items. In the consumer field, it must create a product and a market and, in addition, protect both of these. An understanding of problems involved is essential to the success of any product program.

After association with daily operating problems for a number of years, few individuals can be sure that they can view their problems in broad perspective. The ability to see yourself as others see you is invaluable in growth planning.

In a number of cases, lack of perspective has been the major cause of product program failure. No product stands alone. Each product casts a shadow on other products both in related and nonrelated lines. Perspective is the ingredient in product analysis that makes possible evaluation of these significant product relationships.

"How can perspective be developed?" may be asked. Experience, as well as studying a variety of product development programs and their history, are the only available answers.

Know Your Competition

Product development requires a thorough knowledge of the industry. Familiarity with the state of the art, technology, and trade customs provides the background for evaluating and assaying the soundness of specific product ventures.

Associations and trade councils often provide clearing points for such information. These groups generally are only adequate in part and their work must be supplemented if effective programs are to be achieved.

One corporation follows the practice of assigning to one executive in each major product division the following specific responsibilities. First, he must familiarize himself with the trend of the industry, with particular reference to style, technology, consumer acceptance, and price trends. Second, he must maintain records, including illustrations, trade literature, and operating instructions, covering competitive items. He also has the job of recommending changes, additions, or eliminations affecting the line so that products will have the highest competitive value to the consumer.

Consumer acceptance is the primary and final product criterion. It provides the only commercial and economic basis for justification of product development. These relative values must be weighed in the competitive scale of the market.

Break Away from the Past

Product development should be undertaken in an atmosphere of complete independence with the purpose of achieving certain objectives. Previous methods and ways of doing the job should be cast aside. Attention should be focused on the technical fundamentals and customer requirements involved.

The helicopter resulted from a fundamental study of flight principles and requirements. The jet engine resulted from a similar approach to the aircraft power plant. Today, metal can be cut with a tool, ground with an abrasive, or removed by sparking and electrolysis. All methods are available as a result of fundamental studies of metal removal.

In product development one should begin by learning to forget the past. This advice is not easy to follow. Years of disciplined thinking develop "ruts" that guide thought into well-defined channels. Where this is the case, replacements in the product program staff may be required in order to revive the vitality of the creative thought process.

Protect Product Idea Assets

Product development requires freedom to think, move, and act. It is an exploratory process. Ideas, concepts, and facts must be gathered, catalogued, screened, analyzed, and acted on. The freedom to do these things, however, is not without reservation. Basic ideas must not be revealed and corporate interests should not be disclosed indiscriminately.

Many good ideas have been given away to competitors through carelessness. Product people must be properly trained to respect and protect the idea assets owned by corporations.

This consideration is pointed up by the experience of one corporation where several good product ideas have been lost to competitors. During the exploratory stage competitors learned that engineers were studying certain new product ideas. Competitors liked the idea and moved with more speed, capturing both the idea and the market.

Provide Adequate Facilities

At the outset it is difficult to define plant and facility requirements. Full requirements can't be determined in the early stages. For this reason facilities should be flexible and quickly available. No phase of exploratory programs can safely be neglected simply because of a lack of facilities.

While complete development facilities are costly to maintain—unless they are fully utilized—they are nevertheless essential to the success of any product development undertaking and must be available. Without them, programs repeatedly run into difficulty. One manufacturer had competent engineers but lacked facilities for life-testing final models. The results of the new product venture were disastrous. Shortly after the product was introduced to the market, a design weakness became apparent that made it necessary to recall the product for extensive and costly repairs. It took years for this manufacturer to recover from the loss of trade acceptance suffered as a consequence—"For the lack of a nail, a shoe was lost."

The Job Ahead

Programs should be designed for long-range growth and continuing prosperity. The severe economics of competition face those who attempt the job, so the goal, as always, is to develop sound products in the shortest time and at the lowest cost. Here are ten questions useful in analyzing such programs. Answers to these questions point to strengths and weaknesses, and provide the command of intelligence necessary in product programming.

1. Do we have time to do the job?
2. Do we understand all the problems involved?
3. Do we have the ability (technical knowledge and skills) to tackle product development programming?
4. Do we have the experience necessary?
5. Do we know how to plan a successful product development program?
6. Will we be able to put development programs in their proper perspective?
7. Are we familiar with the practices of our competitors?
8. Can we break away from past practices, concepts, and viewpoints?
9. Are proprietary product ideas protected?
10. Do we have the plant and facilities for product development?

Sound product development programming depends on "yes" answers to all of these questions. Most product programs fail to pass all ten of the tests, but those that do are destined to direct the corporation toward growth.

3

Developing Ideas
for New Products

THE idea that turns out to be the profitable product may be found in any one of many different places. The important thing is to track down the idea wherever it happens to be.

The Nature of "Newness"

To think and act intelligently about ideas for new products, one must understand the concept of new products. A new product is one that meets different needs or reaches different markets from those served by existing products. New products are physical items and services different in nature and purpose from the company's existing products or that incorporate changes of a nature that limit interchangeability with existing products. The new product may be new to the industry, the company, and the consumer, or it may be new to just one of the three. The new product results from new function, better performance, new uses, added function, new markets, lowered cost, upgrading products, downgrading products, and restyling.

New function: Doing things that haven't been done before creates unlimited opportunities. New function results in a readily recognized new product. The development of television provided a function that had not been available previously. Scenes could now be reconstructed electronically at remote points. Videotape, the recording of both black-and-white and color images on tape, provides another new function not available previously.

Better performance: Improved operating characteristics provide new product posture. Better performance results in an essentially new product when the extra increments of performance are such that the potential customer does not regard the product as completely interchangeable with earlier models. For example, the electronic wristwatch, though in outward appearance similar to other wristwatches, operates with greatly improved electromechanical features. An electric battery replaces the mainspring. A tuning fork replaces the balance wheel and escapement. Accuracy within a minute a month is assured. Better performance has resulted in a new product.

New uses: New applications for old products create new markets. The adaptation of existing products in ways that extend their usefulness to new markets results, for all practical purposes, in new products. The aerosol bomb that proved popular as an insecticide spray in its initial use was subsequently adapted to discharge a great variety of other products in a great variety of ways as well as to perform other functions. Among these many uses were applications in the paint, food, and cosmetics industries. It has also been adapted to blow a whistle when room temperatures reach dangerously high levels and to serve as a power source to drive a foghorn. New uses for the television camera have been found in observing industrial operations in dangerous locations and in serving as a silent watchman in banks, stores, and industrial buildings.

Added function: Sales patterns change when products do more than before. The postage meter entered this category when provision was made to print an advertisement at the same time the stamp was printed. Later, another refinement was added—sealing the envelope at the same time it passed through the meter. To the indoor room thermostat, a heat anticipator was added, and later, an outdoor sensing element. A new addition to the telephone permits hands-free operation.

New markets: Tailoring present products to the needs of new consumers opens doors to sales. Present products can be redesigned to extend present functions to new customers. For example, the redesign of the larger "mail room" postage meter for use in the one-man office resulted in a new product for one manufacturer.

Lowered cost: Radical reduction in cost adds new markets. Lowered cost, if great enough, may turn an old idea into a new product. The man-made sapphire is chemically and physically identical to the gem. The new product differs in only one respect—its cost is but a fraction of that of the naturally available product. Now sapphire, which is a structurally hard material, can be used for many applications that cost alone previously prohibited. The synthetic sapphire is used for plug gauges, bearing surfaces, and many other applications for which its chemical and physical properties are uniquely suited. Lowered cost placed the synthetic sapphire in a new product category.

Other cases can be noted. The development of inexpensive electric motors has made it possible to develop battery-powered electrically driven toys. The Model T Ford was, when introduced many years ago, a new product—its lowered cost opened new markets.

Upgrading: End-use applications of present products serve as starting points in planning new product strategy. Present products may be integrated into other products to create new products. For example, one manufacturer of motors used his original product line as a base and developed a new line of kitchen units that included mixers, blenders, and other appliances. A manufacturer of transistors combined his product with capacitors and resistors and created a new line of specialized electronic components.

Downgrading: Purchased parts present product prospects. One manufacturer of television receivers, unable to purchase quality transformers at a satisfactory price, proceeded to manufacture transformers in his own plant. Encouraged by the success of this new product venture, this manufacturer began the production of other components.

Restyling: A "new look" can be a new product. Restyling can turn older products into new products. The new products announced each year in the automobile industry are essentially the result of restyling. The apparel industry provides another example where new products are the result of restyling older products.

Those responsible for developing ideas for new products must understand the scope of newness. To track down new product concepts it's essential to be sensitive to ideas that suggest new function, better performance, new uses, added function, new markets, lowered cost, upgrading products, downgrading products, and restyling. Those responsible for developing ideas for new products must know the nature of newness.

Corporate Interests

In developing new product concepts, certain parameters should be established in keeping with management interests. It is unrealistic to assume that the last-named include any and all potentially profitable new products.

A top level conference, attended by executives responsible for overall company operations, should be held to define top management interests. At this conference, long-range interests should be discussed, as should the thinking behind them. This will enable individuals specifically charged with the task of developing new concepts to exercise judgment in keeping with management thinking.

Management should indicate the limits it wants imposed on the search for new product concepts. Is the sky the limit or is the search limited to cost-reduction concepts? Within this range, practical working parameters can be established. Every effort should be made to allow the fullest possible latitude in searching out new ideas, but if any limitations are imposed by top management, these should be known at the outset. Top management's long-range interests set the ground rules for the search.

The fewer the rules, the greater the chance of success. Complete freedom of operation, however, may suggest that management has not been clear in setting forth its thinking. Trouble may come later when management does clearly delineate its interests.

The greatest contribution management can make at the outset of any search is to pass on knowledge it has of new commercial opportunities that are especially interesting. Through their wide range of contacts, executives can often highlight promising prospects.

The New Product Panel

The search for new product concepts must be pursued inside and outside the corporation with equal vigor. To stimulate the development of new product concepts inside the corporation, the importance of new ideas must be made known. Developing a favorable climate for generating ideas within the corporation requires time and planning. The rewards are great and the results are well worth the time involved.

To gain acceptance of the fact that it is interested in new products, management should make use of written and spoken channels of communication within the corporation. Company publications should carry feature articles outlining the value of new ideas to the long-range growth of the corporation. Reprints of articles from other publications that reveal the importance of new products can help put the point across. Rewards are often used to stimulate a flow of new ideas.

A favorable climate for a free flow of ideas must be maintained. One of the most successful ways of doing this is to establish a new product panel composed of a handpicked group of men charged with the specific responsibility of developing and collecting new product ideas. The most important qualification for members of this group is demonstrated creative ability. Diversity of interests is also important. One such group combines a production expert, an artist, an inventor, a designer, an analyst, and an engineer, all of whom demonstrated creative talent before being selected.

The function of the new product panel is to develop ideas relating to potential products. The function of finding ideas must be clearly disassociated from the function of screening. The new product panel's single responsibility should be to develop the largest possible flow of new product ideas. To operate at maximum effectiveness, it should not concern itself with the screening function. Separating the screening function from that of developing new ideas is fundamental to the success of the process.

As many new ideas as possible must be accumulated; at this point in the process, quantity is the goal. Members of the new product panel should avoid rejecting ideas themselves and should encourage others to submit their ideas without making any attempt to prejudge their merit. Many a man has failed to suggest an idea because he didn't think it would interest management only to discover, later, after someone else suggested the idea, that he had failed to suggest a real winner.

Operating both inside and outside the company, the new product panel is responsible for generating, bird-dogging, and catalyzing new ideas.

Generating Ideas

Members of the panel are specifically charged with a responsibility for generating new product concepts. They are expected to utilize all information that comes to their attention to full advantage in generating new concepts. This job calls for acute awareness, sensitivity, and responsiveness to the slightest hint or suggestion of a potential new product.

The makeup of the new product panel will determine its productivity. Management's principal control is exercised by making certain that the right individuals are selected for the panel. Five attributes have been found to complement each other in the makeup of individuals suited to serve on a new product panel: demonstrated creativity, the ability to associate ideas and facts in new relationships, a questioning approach, acute powers of observation, and the ability to concentrate. No two individuals are alike in the way they combine these attributes.

Demonstrated creativity. Individuals who have performed creative work have learned how to break through emotional, social, and analytical barriers to creative thought processes. They have developed the process of creative thought. Such individuals are outstanding candidates for membership on the new product panel.

Ability to associate ideas and facts in new relationships. The value of an idea is largely a product of its environment. This ability to transplant ideas from a familiar environment into a new one contributes substantially to the output of the panel.

A questioning approach. A mind open to new information quickly detects gaps and uncertainties. Both new information and gaps in established patterns of knowledge are powerful stimulants to the creative thinking process. The man who is always asking questions may have a disquieting influence on those sensitive about not knowing all the answers, but he can make valuable contributions.

Acute powers of observation. An individual's powers of observation are directly related to his ability to assimilate information. Questions open the door to new information, but highly developed powers of observation are essential in collecting and storing new information. The individual who only asks questions, who has not developed the ability to analyze and verify data, will play a lesser role in the activities of the panel.

Ability to concentrate. Those who have the ability to devote their full attention to a subject for long periods of time are particularly productive of new ideas. The ability to concentrate is a basic ingredient of effective action in analyzing relationships, visualizing new associations, and developing new concepts.

The new product panel's ability to generate ideas depends directly on its makeup. If the right people are placed on the panel, productivity is assured. Panel members must therefore be selected with care.

Bird-dogging New Ideas

There are many sources potentially productive of new ideas and ideas that should be tapped. No single listing of these sources could ever be complete, but perhaps some sources will suggest others equally valuable. A partial list of such sources includes

Venture capital organizations seeking corporations interested in financing the development of new products

Directors of research in other corporations with new product ideas available on a royalty basis

Newspapers, trade journals, and magazines revealing new products

Organizations and individuals available to search patent records for ideas that can be developed

Professional societies and business organizations with staff members specializing in certain segments of business activity

Purchasing agents knowing of special market requirements

Inventors with potentially marketable ideas

Public utility companies interested in developing commercial opportunities for their services

Manufacturers' representatives familiar with new developments

Government services related to scientific, industrial, and military activities

City, county, and state industrial development commissions charged with industrial growth of specific areas

Patent attorneys representing client inventors of new products

Trade associations interested in specific areas of industrial activity

Advertising agencies creating merchandising programs for products to be farmed out for manufacturing

Commercial bankers directing the financing of new product activities

Consulting engineers working on projects in the idea and design stage and looking for a commercial tie-in

Sales representatives alert to market needs and potential new developments

Scientists, engineers, and technicians possessing developable ideas

Business acquaintances and personal contacts particularly observant of market needs and opportunities for new industrial ventures

This list may seem exhaustive but a single really good idea is worth a lot of effort, and each of these sources has been found useful on some occasion in the past. Each should therefore be investigated. The sequence followed in exploring these sources will depend on the specialized requirements of a particular search.

Catalyzing a Flow of Ideas

The function of a catalyst is to accelerate a reaction; here the job is to start a flow of new product ideas, especially from those individuals who are in a position to make substantial contributions.

The opportunity of tapping the resources of those directly or indirectly associated with the corporation's activities should not be overlooked. Anyone whose success is related in any way to the success
of the corporation should be willing to make time available to contribute his thinking about possible new product ideas. One of the
new product panel's jobs is to develop and capitalize these resources.

There are many people who can contribute worthwhile ideas. The
people who should be cultivated fall into three categories: those one
sells to (distributors, dealers, and customers), those one buys from
(sales representatives, technical staff members, and executives), and
those one works with (any imaginative individual).

Customers, dealers, and distributors who reach the customers can
contribute valuable ideas when they are approached properly. In the
course of using almost any product, most people will have ideas about
ways the product could be improved. Not only do people have ideas
about particular products, but they think of things they might like
to see on the market. These ideas are worth something to alert manufacturers. It is not easy to get a total stranger to take time to give
one the benefit of his thinking, but if it's gone about in the right
way, it can be done. The company's customers, however, are not
strangers. They have a stake in the success and the growth of business
and can help themselves get better products in the long run by taking
time out to pass their ideas along.

Suppliers are in a similar position. From time to time, vendor's
executives, technical staff members, and sales representatives develop
product opportunities they don't intend to exploit themselves. These
may turn out to be particularly interesting. Certainly they are worth
reviewing. Finally, closest to home, are the employees of the firm—
from the office boy to the board of directors.

Tapping the Source

To stimulate a flow of ideas from these sources requires three
things: Show people how ideas are important to themselves as well
as to the corporation, invite people to submit ideas, and maintain
a climate favorable to the flow of ideas. The future of those associated
in any way with the firm's business is inseparably linked to the future
of the firm itself. A simple request for assistance should be sufficient
to enlist cooperation. Many competent people are timid about offering
opinions unless specifically asked for them. They may have been re-
buffed too often in the past when they have offered unsolicited sugges-

tions. In the search for product ideas and suggestions, a very clear and pointed request for help must be made.

In asking others for their suggestions, the following ten points are well worth keeping in mind.

1. Do not criticize, qualify, or express reservations about the suggestions offered.
2. Acknowledge every suggestion as one having potential merit.
3. Encourage wild ideas.
4. Find an opportunity to read into the suggestion possible combinations and improvements.
5. Give credit for ideas suggested.
6. Ask for expansion of suggestions.
7. Keep ideas flowing—avoid discussion of technical details.
8. Compliment productivity.
9. Reflect enthusiasm.
10. Show appreciation.

As part of a longer-range program, formalized educational programs can be set up to develop creative thinking in both the individual and the group. The results of such programs have proved rewarding.

Idea Development—a Management Responsibility

Products have varying life-spans that can be projected with reasonable accuracy. Such projections serve to emphasize the necessity of ideas for new products. Developing them is one of management's most important responsibilities in corporations where the emphasis is on growth, stability, and increased profits.

4

Picking
Profitable Products

AN executive who spent his early years in a racetrack town once remarked that picking product winners is a lot like picking turf winners. Both require horse sense. Of course, winners may be picked by luck, but the odds favor the seasoned veteran who can draw on knowledge and experience.

Sound product lines make sound business. Stability and growth depend on sound product lines. "For Rent or Sale" signs are soon nailed to factory buildings when managers fail in their job of picking profitable products.

A knowledge and understanding of what's important in picking product winners can be acquired. This essential knowledge isn't the private property of a select few; it's available to anyone. But its acquisition demands time and attention—indeed too much of both, for some. Over the years new product successes and failures have made available a large amount of data that is instructive in avoiding pitfalls.

Managers must think in broad economic terms. It is just as important to select products having an economically justified end use as it is to design products in an economical manner. Managers must apply the same orderly analytical process in studying end-use requirements that they apply in the design of products to satisfy these needs. Recognizing the need for and applying this orderly process brings out the latent horse sense that has proved so valuable to those who have been successful at picking winners.

After time and money have been spent developing what proves to be the wrong product, it is too late to do much about it. On the other hand, care in screening and appraising potential new products can eliminate costly failures. It is impossible to calculate the full cost of a single product failure. Involved are both direct cost—items such as development expense—and indirect costs—such intangibles as lowered morale. And beyond these is the loss of the profits that more than likely would have accompanied a successful new product.

There is still another important aspect. Not long ago an executive remarked, "We have never introduced a new product that wasn't a success." His firm is to be congratulated if it has not passed over better products—products that would have been even more successful than the ones introduced. Unrealized profits represent losses just as real as any other.

The Mousetrap Fallacy

The selection of sound product concepts starts with what might seem to be a backward step. One must progress through an unlearning phase: Fallacious ingrained concepts must be cleared away.

Men have been told that if they build a better mousetrap than their competitor, customers will beat a path to their door. This is nonsense. Such thinking by managers has probably caused more business headaches and heartaches than any other single factor. Sales are made when customers want a better mousetrap and are willing to pay for it.

Managers are inclined to look at product design from the viewpoint of customers' needs. But customers think in terms of wants, not needs. Joe Doe may not need a new ball-point pen, but if he wants one, a potential sale is created for the manufacturer who has a new pen to offer.

Sales are made by satisfying wants, not needs. Many years ago one leading automobile manufacturer learned at disastrous expense that the need for an automobile incorporating airflow styling did not coincide with the then current wants of customers.

In picking new products, pick products that give customers what they want. Don't limit thinking to technical requirements. This is much too narrow a base.

The price a customer is willing to pay is the significant price in evaluating new products. Pricing related to costs does not take into consideration what the customer is willing to pay. A clear understanding of this latter figure is vital.

A man may not need a $15 pen—a dollar pen may be adequate—but his willingness to pay the higher price creates a market. Low-priced electric motors may cost more in the long run than higher priced motors, but unless customers are willing to pay the higher price, no real market exists for the higher priced product.

Some argue that when customers don't want what they really need and aren't willing to pay a price they can't afford not to pay, customers should be "educated." It takes both time and money to do this job. In the interim, sales are lost to those who offer customers what they want.

The mousetrap fallacy results from a confusion of the real significance of wants, needs, and willingness to pay. A thorough knowledge of its implications is important. Until this fallacy is recognized and understood, one can't pick profitable products. The fallacy points up the importance of three questions pertinent to sound product programs. What do customers want? What are they willing to pay? Can it be provided at an attractive profit? The search for answers to these questions is not an easy task, but a systematic approach will help.

Appraising New Product Ideas

When one begins to ask questions about the mechanics by which particular ideas are selected for further development work, many times he learns that ideas are selected on the basis of intuition or "hunch." When attempting to probe what underlies them, one usually encounters mental fogginess. Some successful managers find that much of their so-called intuition rests on a basis no firmer than a coin-tossing decision, backed up only by opinion and force. In sharp contrast with such decisions is the practice of those who have a highly developed fact-gathering process and an analytical procedure for screening and appraising ideas.

Some have been extremely successful in gambling on ideas for new products, but the risks involved in such gambles are much too great for sound long-range planning purposes. Admittedly, most business decisions incorporate certain elements of chance, but there is no valid reason for extending the gamble into areas where decisions can be based on facts. A systematic appraisal program for new product ideas is based on five fundamental steps:

1. Define the product concept.
2. Eliminate ideas unacceptable to management.

3. Investigate technical-economic aspects.
4. Review the literature.
5. Appraise and evaluate.

Product programs have sometimes failed because a single step in this process was overlooked. Each step, and the order in which the steps are taken, is important. Each step must be given careful attention as the basis for the next step.

The Product Concept

As product ideas are accumulated, they should be translated into product concepts. Preparatory to evaluation, each idea should be given definition in the form of a descriptive title and a concise statement of the scope of the idea and its use. These questions, then, must first be asked: What does the new product idea contribute by way of new or improved function or lowered cost? How is this contribution accomplished? What alternatives exist? Why was the proposed method selected?

A clear definition of the product concept establishes parameters for idea evaluation. At this point, definition is given to the idea. Prior to this, the product idea has been nebulous. To be considered further, the idea must be put in a form understandable to others who may make valuable contributions to its success.

The presentation of an idea, no matter how good it is, is liable to encounter closed minds if it is not handled properly. The individual who initially develops an idea has usually given it a lot of thought. In his own mind, he has asked and answered many questions before giving it his personal stamp of approval. Indeed, he should not expect others to accept it without the benefit of this background of exploratory analysis.

Further preliminary analysis of the proposed product should be based on the statement of the product concept. Further qualification of the idea may be needed as the screening process unfolds, but the statement of the product concept should anticipate as many of these questions as possible.

The Unacceptable Idea

Management generally has more or less well-defined interests. An idea may be unacceptable simply because management is interested in a different line of business. For example, a control equipment manufacturer turned down a well-defined idea for a revolutionary water softener on one occasion, and an idea for a new machine tool on another, simply because the proposals represented radical departures from the company's established business.

The scope of established corporate interests is determined by management thinking and by the legal parameters that govern the activities of most businesses. The articles of incorporation contain a statement of the company's purposes. The stated purposes have a direct bearing on product programs. Corporation charters may, of course, be amended, but such action must be explored by the corporation's attorneys prior to any large expenditure of time or money on ideas that fall outside the corporation's stated purposes.

The general provisions as to the purposes of the corporation are sometimes stated in language broad enough to cover practically all kinds of business. One corporation, for example, is empowered to buy, sell, produce, manufacture, and dispose of all kinds of goods, wares, foods, potables, drugs, merchandise, manufactures, commodities, furniture, machinery, agricultural tools, supplies and products, and generally to engage in and conduct any form of manufacturing or mercantile enterprise not contrary to law. In sharp contrast, the stated purpose of another corporation is limited to the manufacturing of lampblack, carbon black, gas black, and kindred tar-oil products and to buy and sell the same. The scope of the corporation, obviously, may be broad or narrow.

No idea should get past initial screening that management will not or cannot support. Ideas should be sifted so as to remove from further consideration those that will not win management acceptance.

The Technical–Economic Analysis

A technical–economic evaluation seems to call for doing the impossible in the shortest possible time. To accept this is to be in the right frame of mind for the preliminary analysis of a proposed new product's chances for success. Naturally, such an evaluation calls for a lot of calculated guesses. Yet in retrospect, however random it may seem, guessing does incorporate available facts having a bearing on the situation. Beyond this, guessing should be so organized that aggregated guesses serve as checks and balances.

Product ideas can be better evaluated later, after further definition and development. The fact remains that further definition and development cost more time and money. The purpose of the preliminary analysis is to substitute brainpower for time and money and thereby bring into focus commercially feasible ideas.

Somewhat oversimplified, a technical–economic evaluation of a new product idea has as its object the answering of two questions: Can it be made? Can it be sold at a profit? As soon as these questions are answered, the evaluation has served its purpose. The first question relates directly to the technical feasibility of the idea and takes into consideration research, development, production, marketing, installation, and servicing. The second question relates to an analysis of the economic feasibility of the investment. In answering these two major questions nine other basic questions must be asked.

1. What is the outlook for the industry identified with the proposed product? A clue to the probable success of any product can be found in the outlook for the industry the product will enter if put on sale. For example, to introduce an automatic control that will be installed primarily on milling machines, get a picture of the outlook for the entire machine tool industry, along with the milling machine segment. Before giving serious consideration to a new product, a comprehensive knowledge of its industry should be developed.

You may want to place the product on the market even when the industry doesn't show signs of healthy growth or even when there are definite signs of industry decline, but sound judgment dictates adapting product lines to healthy industries. In making an analysis of the industry, pertinent questions must be asked and answered.

Annual industry sales should be explored with such questions as: How large is the industry? What volume of business does this type of product represent within the industry? What volume of business could be derived from this specific product? About current industry trends, one should ask: What has taken place in research, engineering, manufacturing, sales, finance, and distribution? Finally, one should ask: What is the outlook for the industry?

2. What are the important features of the proposed product? To pick a profitable product one must "know" each product in the group from which the selection is to be made. Knowing implies an understanding of more than surface characteristics.

The proposed product must be seen in its most significant perspective—its ability to perform. Forget loyalty to pet projects. Examine product proposals critically, without bias.

These are also important questions: What does the product provide in the way of new function, improved function, and lower costs? How does it relate to: economy, health, appearance, safety, labor savings, time savings, and comfort? Is this the best way we know to accomplish these objectives? If not, what is the best way? Why not adopt that? Is this the lowest cost method of accomplishing these objectives? If not, what is the lowest cost approach? Why not adopt that? Is there any installation problem? If so, what is it? If so, how much of a sales deterrent is it? What are the principal weaknesses of the proposed product? How important are these as sales deterrents? What modifications are needed for better performance, design, capacity, and simplicity? What modifications are required to meet "approval" requirements? How important and how costly are these modifications? What should be done to improve sales appeal, styling, weight, size, and adaptability in order to reduce the operating cost and to increase safety? What can be done to increase capacity and to simplify design and operation? Should further technical tests be made before test sales campaigns? What tests? Why? What will they cost and how long will they take?

3. *How do patents and licenses affect introduction of the product?* Patent and licensing relationships should be thoroughly reviewed. Has the door been closed by existing patents to any consideration of the particular product other than by agreement with the patent owner? Do patents provide adequate protection? To what extent are present manufacturers infringing? What special agreements or contracts have been made? Do any obligations exist? Is it probable that it would be more economical, in both time and money, to develop an equivalent, patent-free device? Does cross-licensing seem feasible or desirable? What would necessary patent rights cost?

4. *What effect will the proposed product have on relationships growing out of other products offered to the trade?* Products influence the makeup of all corporate relationships. Once a line of products becomes established, its active part in these relationships becomes so familiar it is not recognized. The product line is part of an established system. The introduction of any new product carries with it the necessity of a series of adjustments.

Here too, questions must be asked. Does this product eliminate or reduce the market for any existing product? Does the required new method of operation conflict with other methods of the firm? Would entry into the proposed product area jeopardize the management's or the stockholders' interests in any way? Would community relationships be affected? Is the net incidental effect favorable?

5. *What is the market for the product?* A market appraisal is one of the vital steps in product selection. The relative potential strength of the market for various products under consideration will

modify the importance of other factors such as patents and product characteristics.

For example, with adequate patent protection, a relatively limited market can prove attractive even where profit margins are slim because the risk is made negligible by the protective patent coverage. To illustrate again, where other product lines make available both a sales and service force, a marginal market for a new product may prove of interest. The cost of tapping this market would be nominal.

Market appraisals must be comprehensive. The true significance of data will be revealed only after a survey of all factors. The pertinent questions are these: What are customer characteristics? Does the market vary greatly geographically? How? What list price is necessary to secure volume? How will operating costs influence the market? What is the life of the product? What is the life of the market? What is the degree of market saturation? What are the estimated sales by years? When is the optimum time to strike the market? How soon can the item be placed on the market?

6. *How should the product be distributed?* Neither the soundness of a product nor the existence of a market for it guarantees that it will be economically feasible to reach the people who want the product, with the product, at the point of sale. Distribution factors must be surveyed to establish the probable degree of success of the proposed product. For example, in evaluating a new industrial motor you must know that a large proportion of industrial motor sales are made directly to equipment manufacturers. Successful introduction of a new motor requires a staff that can reach these equipment manufacturers. Other products have slightly differing but equally important requirements that must be considered.

You can't afford to neglect a study of the characteristics of the particular distribution system required by each product under review. A product can't be sold unless a customer is contacted. This is the job the distribution program performs in the success or failure of a new product offering. Questions to ask include these: Should preliminary market tests be made? Does the retail sale involve engineering, contracting, or other special ability? What channels seem best fitted to sell the product? Can demand be increased by low-price introductory sales offers? Should they be made? To whom? How? At what cost? In what section or department of the company does the product belong now? Why? In what section or department of the company does the product belong eventually? Why? If seasonal sales appeals vary, what action must be taken to meet these situations?

7. *What competition can be anticipated?* To evaluate product pro-

posals, you must know first, the product, and second, the competition. Any product's success or failure is determined at least partly by its competition, and therefore it must be examined. Who are the competitors? How important are they? What are their practices?

Not the least important consideration is this: What time period would be required to get on the market with a competitive product? The answer should reveal the competitive risk associated with the product offering. For example, consider the relative risk in market entry by a new steel producer as contrasted with market entry by a new machine shop, food processor, or cosmetics distributor. The first would take years, the others months. In the former the competitive picture is free from the risk of precipitous shifts; in the latter, the picture can change overnight.

The competition's strength and stability must be assessed. Changes in the status quo can seriously affect profit ratios. Managers must ask: Would we be competitive—in price? Efficiency? Operating cost? Capacity? Value? What product improvements are competitors likely to initiate? How long would it take a competitor to put a product on the market? How can active or potential competition be effectively overcome?

8. *What are the estimated costs and potential profits?* Everything up to this point has been deliberately designed to develop a background for cost studies. The importance of cost exerts a pressure upon men for premature figures. When men succumb to these pressures they should remember that errors in calculations are remembered long after the contributing pressures have been forgotten.

It is the cost man's duty to call attention to the importance of adequate basic data as a foundation for cost estimates. If he fails in this, the cost man must accept contributory responsibility for the consequences of cost estimates that are not reliable guides. The cost man must ask such questions as: What are the costs to get into business on a continuing basis? What are the unit costs? What is the selling price? When will sales volume liquidate costs to date plus interest on the investment? Does price show long-range stability? If not, how will it influence profits? How many years will be required to achieve a relatively stable profit position? Over this period, how much will the cost, out of pocket, represent in total dollars? Does the venture seem to offer good profit potentials?

9. *How much of a threat does technological development present?* Technological development plays a dual role. It is a source of new products and at the same time a constant threat to new products— it may make them obsolete before they appear on the market. In

evaluating a new product proposal one must not only look at the potential for the product but also appraise the threat of early obsolescence from subsequent technological development. Rapidly advancing technology can shorten a new product's life-span to the point where it will be impossible to recover the investment.

The technological obsolescence threat is two-pronged. Advanced designs may make the product unsalable. New developments in other technologies may cause a market shift.

Managers must exercise their imagination in probing research and development activities for clues to new developments that can have a significant impact on product proposals under review. The overall objective of the technical-economic analysis is to establish the relative commercial feasibility of the idea at the earliest possible moment, with a minimum expenditure of development time and money.

The Literature Study

Valuable resource material for product analysis has been developed by trade association groups, professional societies, government agencies, and individual corporations. In addition, there are the continuing contributions of those working in specific areas of specialization. One must not make the mistake of thinking that because material is available without charge it is without value. Some of the most authoritative technological and industrial writing is available at little or no cost because its preparation and publication costs are absorbed by a corporation or other groups as a service gesture. Some of the best material merits such sponsorship.

Literature reviews should be made on a continuing basis. As specific product ideas come under consideration, literature studies should be intensified. The development of the transistor, large-scale integration, and monolithic memory array changed a lot of thinking in the electronics industry. Those who kept up with the literature could have sufficiently anticipated these developments to incorporate them in long-range planning. Technological developments, economic trends, and news of the business community have a direct bearing on product decisions. All of these are part of the background for analysis and decision making.

One very important value of the literature study lies in the fact that it affords the best opportunity of gathering background data without tipping one's hand to a competitor. Almost any other approach to data gathering introduces the risk of revealing specific interests.

Beyond this, when close contact with the literature is not maintained, decisions are usually made in an information vacuum. The skilled analyst is one who has learned how to keep in touch with significant literature that bears directly on operations. By keeping abreast of developments, he can separate specious statements from penetrating analysis. If the analyst is willing to take the time to personally check some of the information culled from the literature, he can operate with reasonable assurance that he has a sound basis for decision.

The failure to review literature on a continuing basis will almost certainly result in the loss of valuable data. At the very least, it will mean the data will cost more to acquire. In either event, the process of screening and appraising product ideas will be seriously impaired.

Appraisal and Evaluation

Once the facts have been corralled, they must be used as a basis for decision and action. Essentially, this is a process of adding up the plus and minus signs.

First, it is important to check all essential information for accuracy and to assemble it for effective presentation. Management time is too valuable to be wasted on a morass of detail. There is no greater deterrent to effective executive action than the absence of adequate, streamlined data.

Second, it is important to bring together everyone who should play a part in a new product decision. Personal bias in decision making can be reduced if individuals are called on to justify their reasoning in the presence of others who play a contributory role in the decision-making process.

Third, the evaluation process deals exclusively in the selection of alternative courses of action based on relative values. Formulas are not workable. There are no established criteria universally applicable. Keep in mind that decisions can be no better than the best alternative available at the time of decision making.

Decision and Action

This step opens the door to the expenditure of substantial sums of money for research and commercial development of ideas that are accepted. Decision and action call for an appraisal of the future, where the commercial life of new products lies. Decisions cannot be expected to guarantee successful end products. Even an established product's future cannot be projected with any accuracy, and the intangible nature of ideas makes predicting their course even more difficult.

Decision and action must be based first of all on bringing together significant facts. But all pertinent opinions, as well as all pertinent facts, must be reflected in the decisions reached. This is the only basis for effective action in picking profitable products.

5

Pricing New Products

PRICING new products should begin when the first tentative specification for a new product is established. As the tentative specification is turned into physical hardware, new concepts will alter specifications. In turn, price and cost projections will influence design.

Since we are all customers for many products ourselves, let's consider our own reactions as a starting point and look at some typical purchasing decisions. All of us have decided on one occasion or another that a particular product was too expensive. We decided that some other product was a good buy, that another was something we wanted regardless of price, and that still other products were ones we wouldn't want at any price.

For example, we may look at a color television receiver selling for roughly $500 and decide it isn't worth it to be able to receive a color picture.

We may see an imported English meerschaum selling at a special price of $2 and decide that although we hadn't planned to buy a meerschaum, the price is too good to turn down.

Having contracted a virus infection we take a prescription to the pharmacy and purchase an antibiotic preparation without considering the price. Afterthoughts about the price are immaterial because we have made our purchase.

In a music-store window we see a harp selling for $3,000. Even if the price were just $30 we wouldn't buy it.

In the face of this, how do we arrive at guidelines for pricing a new product?

First, observe that buying decisions are influenced in varying degrees by actual needs and by personal reactions to the price. It is improbable that customers are concerned with the manufacturer's cost of producing the product, whether his cost was 10 percent or 90 percent of the selling price. Think in terms of retail prices, not manufacturing costs.

What about the purchaser of industrial items? What decisions must be made to authorize the purchase of raw materials and components? In most cases, specifications are established before bids are solicited. Factors such as low price, ability to meet delivery dates, and reputation for maintaining quality are some of the final determinants.

There are three categories of industrial products: (1) highly competitive products, such as nuts, screws and bolts, steel, radio tubes, and paint; (2) radically new products, such as an atomic-powered cell for portable radios; (3) specialty products supplied by a single source.

How do purchasers react to the prices of products in each of these categories? In purchasing highly competitive products such as steel, the purchasing decision is seldom, if ever, influenced by price. Regardless of the supplier, the price will be the same.

For pricing purposes, radically new products and specialty products can be considered together. In almost every case, the radically new product is offered by a single supplier. If this product can be protected by patents or other methods, the supplier who introduces the product will at least for a time remain the single source of supply. As a result, the radically new product and the specialty product can be regarded as different points in the product life-span.

The usual assumption is that the supplier has complete control over the price of this radically new product. Assume further that a high price can be placed on a new product. This will result in high initial profits, but will attract competition. On the other hand, a low price will result in the most rapid acceptance of a new product by the market. Assume further that this low price will increase the period of time taken to recover development costs, but will discourage competitors from entering the field. Another assumption is that a low-price policy should be followed if one of the primary purposes of the new product is its complementary effect on the product line.

All this is unrealistic for a number of reasons. First, both the producer of the new product and those who might be lured into competition will be concerned with profits over a period of years. No one is so naive as to think that initial-offering prices won't change.

For this reason, the supposed effect of a high price in encouraging competition, or a low price in discouraging competition, can be discounted. Profit-minded business managers are going to look at the long-term picture.

Second, the concept of a high price or a low price can exist only with respect to a base line. Here, the base line is the cost of producing the new product. At the outset of commercial production, no one can be certain about the cost of production. No one can be sure of sales volume. As experience is gained, engineering and production techniques are constantly improving, and costs are reduced.

For example, in the early days of the electric blanket, one of the elements of cost was a relatively expensive transformer that changed the higher voltage house current to the lower voltage on which the electric blanket operated. Subsequent production techniques lowered costs by eliminating this expensive transformer so the blanket could operate at the voltage of the household supply.

Third, the volume factor creates another unknown element in calculating profitability. Sales volume is the multiplier of the profit margin. It determines total profit levels.

Pricing Strategy

The objective is to establish a price within a range where sales wouldn't increase substantially if prices were lowered, and would fall off rapidly if prices were raised; see Exhibit 1.

It's generally assumed that as unit selling prices are increased, sales volume falls off proportionately, and as unit selling prices are decreased, sales volume increases proportionately.

If this were true, pricing would be a simple matter. One would merely find the point where price-profit relationships are optimum by calculating potential sales volume for each different price increment. As unit prices are increased, the assumed volume decrease would increase unit costs and decrease unit profit, thereby offsetting increased prices.

It isn't safe to assume that sales volume will respond to price changes according to this model. Experience has shown that price changes sometimes have effects directly opposite to those that might be expected. The pricing of either consumer or industrial products at too low a level may result in their being regarded as inferior products by potential customers.

Reversing the process, on the other hand, can be profitable. By increasing the price per yard of a particular fabric to 20 times its original price, it was possible to move the fabric from an economy-product category to a prestige-product category with a substantial increase in yardage sales volume and an even greater increase in dollar volume.

Nearest Equivalent Product

The important point in pricing is to determine in advance the value the customer will place on the product. This approach may not appear objective, but it can't be denied that the customer is the one who decides to buy or not to buy. The price of a new product, to be realistic, must be decided from the customer's viewpoint.

A helpful guide is to recognize that the customer is a comparison

---

Exhibit 1. Price-profit relationships.

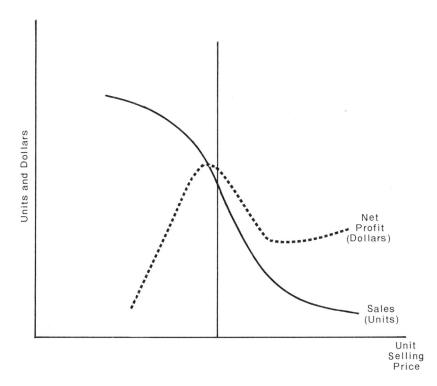

shopper. Regardless of product, the customer will compare your price with the price of a familiar product, that is, a Nearest Equivalent Product (NEP).

Some of these NEP's are so similar that they require little guesswork by those responsible for pricing new products. If you are introducing a new loaf of bread of more or less conventional quality there is little question that the customer will compare this with other loaves of bread on the grocer's shelf.

A classic example, some years back, was the pricing of the original Reynolds ball-point pen. Because of its advantages over the fountain pen, the ball-point pen was priced considerably above even the better fountain pens then on the market. It was felt that customers would value the ball-point's special features, particularly in a wartime period, when novel gift items were scarce.

In other cases, what the customer will regard as the NEP requires considerable ingenuity to detect.

If you are pricing a new kind of sailboat to be sold to a market made up of those who haven't been able to afford the pleasure of sailing, the NEP your customer may use for comparison purposes might be the price he pays for golf during an entire season—a sport he might abandon for sailing.

If a solar-powered motor is being introduced to a manufacturer, his NEP concept may include his present power source, its components, and its cost of maintenance.

Determining the product the customer will establish as the NEP is the starting point in pricing new products. The next step is to position the new product relative to this nearest equivalent on a value scale.

The Pricing Profile

Once an idea for a new product has been related to its nearest equivalent from the customer's viewpoint, it must be related to its nearest equivalent on a performance and group-appeal scale.

Assume that an atomic-powered digital clock is to be introduced. Potential customers will immediately compare this proposed clock with other clocks on the market. The NEP is already established, but there are two more questions: Will the proposed product offer better performance? To what customers will the product have greatest group appeal?

From a pricing position, performance and group-appeal measures provide the best guidelines possible. They are not as exact as engineers would like, but they do point a direction.

In the case of an atomic-powered clock, there are a number of advantages. The clock would not require an electrical outlet. Mounted on the wall, it would have no unsightly wire dangling from it. A small model could be carried as a travel clock, and would operate continuously without winding.

Beyond these advantages, the product concept might be adapted to a chime clock. Further, a model might be designed to show day of the week, the date, and phase of the moon. An alarm might be added and a recorded voice tell the time. It could also turn on radio or television.

At the opposite extreme, the design might be greatly simplified if there were a market for a very low-priced clock. Certain products may appeal to different markets at different points along both the prestige scale and the value scale.

A single product price might be high for consumers and low for industrial customers.

Consider another idea for a new product—a device that would indicate temperature at a remote point. Such a device might consist of two units. One would have a temperature-indicating scale and could be mounted on any wall since no wiring would be required. The other unit, also self-contained, could be placed anywhere within a radius of 1,000 feet of the indicating unit. This second temperature-sensing and -transmitting unit could be located either indoors or outdoors. At a glance, the owner of this device could tell the temperature at the point where the transmitting unit was located. Fifty feet of waterproof wire attached to the sensing unit would enable the temperature-sensing element to be located under water, underground, or in a processing bath.

A product of this type might be expected to have two markets—industrial and consumer. In the consumer market, this product would take on a definite prestige character at a high price. It might be used by an estate owner to indicate the temperature of a lake. Or it might be used at some open spot on the property to indicate the prevailing temperature. The indoor-outdoor thermometer would be its NEP. As an industrial item in a market where similar products are already used, the device might be developed to be priced far below existing equipment.

The two scales, performance and group appeal, used in making the price profile, are also useful in positioning price with reference to the nearest equivalent product.

What's It Worth?

It may be disturbing to come this far and to hear no mention of cost. But what does cost have to do with price? Not much. The difference between price and cost is profit, but price and cost aren't directly related. Their makeup involves different factors.

A producer may have a number of objectives. He wants to establish product acceptance. He wants to recover his development and production costs. He wants to make a profit. He wants both a long-range and a short-range profit. He wants the product to increase the acceptance of his other products. He wants to discourage competition.

But if he is to price a product realistically, his primary objective must be to determine the values that consumers will attach to the product. Any attempt at a pricing decision based primarily on the desires of the producer will result in frustration. Price is determined by the customer on the basis of his own answer to the question "What's it worth?"

6

Projecting
the Profitability
of New Products

EACH company has a makeup all its own—it is different from any other company. Its executives work together in their own individual way, set apart from all other company groups. A company also has special characteristics—a "company personality"—when viewed through the eyes of its customers, based on the record built up over the years regarding quality, service, price, manner of doing business, and the like, all of which will have a bearing on customer expectations with respect to any new products brought to the market. Management consultants who are brought in on some phase of new product development frequently find that a management has difficulty in seeing its company as others see it. Yet if management is to make sound decisions on new products, its company operations must be viewed in such a perspective.

A wealth of information can be drawn from the company's history, which can then be used to develop guidelines for evaluating new product programs. Probing questions must be asked to furnish clues as to what to expect in the future. Unless there has been a radical change in the management makeup of a company or in the nature of its markets, it is a pretty safe bet that future operations will be carried out very much as they have been in years past. This does not mean that a company is always going to be satisfied doing things as it has always done them; but in the absence of the type of shake-up mentioned, changes are apt to come slowly, and the innovator will have to push his ideas vigorously.

Ten Critical Factors in Product Choice

Decisions regarding product and project choices cannot, of course, be better than the alternatives presented. Ten critical profitability factors must be considered in narrowing the choice from among the products and projects that have passed prior exploration and screening.

Profit versus Investment

Each new product a company adds to its line ties up or uses up part of the company's resources. In return—it is hoped—sales of each new product will add to overall profit. By calculating the ratio of this profit return to the associated investment for each proposed product, one gets a picture of the relative contribution it makes to overall company profits in relation to the share of the company's assets tied up by it.

Management must think of each product as the basis of a small business and ask such questions as: How much factory or processing plant is required to produce the product? What portion of the company's equipment and tools are used for it? What portion of the company's working capital is needed to keep this product in the company's catalog? Answers will reveal the gross operating investment allocated to a particular product. After the return on investment ratios are calculated for each proposed product, these can be ranked in order, from high to low, to highlight their relative profitability as compared with the profitability of existing products.

Some will argue that one cannot divide up the company's investment in a plant, machines, and other elements of the operating investment on a product basis. Admittedly the job is not easy and some compromises will have to be made, but in the final analysis the income from the sale of the company's products must, in one way or another, justify all money tied up in their production. If, for example, the company's regular products return a profit of between 10 and 15 percent on the gross operating investment allocated to each, it cannot be assumed without proof that a proposed product will turn in a better performance. A new product cannot be expected to overcome the built-in operating and performance levels of the various functions involved unless more persuasive facts can be presented.

In using return-on-investment measures, it is necessary to keep in mind the magnitude of the gross operating investment and return for each product, as well as the ratios. One can be misled by percentages alone. For example, a 50 percent return on a $10,000 investment is only a $5,000 annual contribution to the company's overall profits; a return of only 10 percent on a $200,000 investment represents a $20,000 contribution. Decisions will depend on company policy. Here the $10,000 project, though highly profitable, would probably be considered too trivial by a large company, and the 10 percent return on the larger project inadequate. Return on investment must thus be viewed in the light of the investment base, and the cut-off point in profit return below which no projects will be considered.

Development Time

How long will it take to turn an idea into dollars—profit dollars? Again, what has been done in the past, unless persuasive facts and plans can be adduced to the contrary, serves as a pretty good indication of what will be done in the future. How long did it take to turn previous ideas into today's products? Detailed analysis of past performance records does a lot to clear the air with respect to the reasonableness of present and projected development projects. Management is always prone to feel that development departments take too long to get new products ready for production . . . or production departments to get new items into the hands of the sales force . . . or sales people to get products into an established position in the market. It is probably true that almost everyone could do a better job, but the starting point in any planning process lies in the development of a clear and unvarnished picture of the historical record.

There is a best time to hit the market with any new product. In some cases, the sooner the better, since no one can be sure what competitors will do. However, there are times when the best course of action is to let others pioneer the market and educate customers to the need for a new type of product. Obviously a realistic projection of development time is vital to the timing of market introduction, and the research manager must work closely with the market-analysis manager and the sales manager.

Development Cost

Development time and development cost must be considered together. It is often assumed that crash programs are the most costly of all. Those who think so had better check their figures to make sure. This may be the least costly type of program to conduct. The apparent savings from seemingly greater efficiency in scheduling development work over a longer period may be more than offset by the cost of moneys tied up during the extra time involved, and, probably more importantly, by the loss of sales and market position that could have been attained had the product been available earlier.

Cost of Capital

The cost of money allocated to any development must be kept in mind, and research planners must develop the habit of viewing proposed projects through the eyes of financial planners. For example, a development project may call for an expenditure of $10,000 a year for five years, with an extra $10,000 put in at the start. Over a five-year period a total of $60,000 will have been invested. This money must come from somewhere. If the company borrows the money, it will have to pay interest on it. If the company makes the funds available from money that would otherwise have gone into its regular business, its money cost will be the return it would normally have made from such an expansion of existing operations.

One method analysts use in judging the financial attractiveness (or lack of attractiveness) of a new project is to compare the projected profit with the return that would accrue if the same amount of money were invested in the regular business (or, for the sake of argument, in bonds or other investments yielding the same return as the regular business), taking into consideration the time over which the money inputs will have to be spread and the time periods in which the profits will be forthcoming——since there will usually be a more or less extensive development period before any returns are realized.

Referring to the above-mentioned project calling for an expenditure of $10,000 a year for five years, after the start-up, the present value of this outgoing cash flow can be calculated by making use of a "discounted cash flow" table. If the company's return on money used in the business is 8 percent after taxes, or if that is management's goal, then the desired alternative return on money put into new projects is minimally 8 percent also (but should actually be greater or why go into what may be a risky new venture?). If, instead of putting money into the new project it is possible to invest $10,000 a year in something giving 8 percent return, then the present cost of $10,000 invested annually for six years is $49,926, as can be seen from Table 1. In other words, if you needed $10,000 at the end of the first year, you would need only $9,259 today, since that sum, invested at 8 percent, would provide you with $10,000 a year later. The same reasoning, using compound interest at 8 percent, would give the present cost of $10,000 needed two years hence, three years hence, and so on, as shown in Table 1.

The net outlays and net proceeds associated with any product development form the cash flow into and out of the program. In practically every case an outlay is made at intervals over a period of years. Similarly, proceeds are returned over time intervals. Discounted cash-flow analysis takes account of timing and interest rates by putting everything on a "present value" basis.

A clarification regarding "present cost" of moneys needed later may be in order here. To someone not accustomed to this form of financial analysis, it may seem odd to say that if he requires $10,000 a year from today for his new project, its "cost" to him as of today is only $9,259. If he has to borrow money when the time comes to apply it to the project, he may argue that the cost of the money will be 5 percent or whatever interest rate he may have to pay in the light of his own standing as a credit risk to a bank or other source of funds. But remember that one is comparing the new project, proposed to be initiated today, with a hypothetical alternative investment opportunity, presumed to be readily available, returning

Table 1. Present value of future outlays at 8 percent, compounded annually.

End of Year	Projected Outlay	Discount Factor	Present Value of Net Outlay
0 (Start)	$10,000	1.0000	$10,000
1	10,000	.9259	9,259
2	10,000	.8573	8,573
3	10,000	.7938	7,938
4	10,000	.7350	7,350
5	10,000	.6806	6,806
	$60,000		$49,926

A total of $49,926 invested on an 8 percent return basis would provide a cash flow of $60,000 over a five-year period to finance the project, with $10,000 put in at the very start. Comparison of the present value of net outlay of alternative proposals allows for the effect of the timing factor on future expenditures, and considers the cost of the capital required as the earning rate of the capital if it were invested in the regular business.

8 percent. One is, so to speak, imagining himself standing at the beginning of the project with enough liquid funds in his hands to finance the whole project over the ensuing years, and also assuming that he has a choice as to where to put that money—into the new project or into the 8 percent investment opportunity. Even if he decides to go ahead with the new project, he nevertheless theoretically invests all of the money in the 8 percent investment, except for what is needed at any time for the new project, which is drawn out as required. That is why it can be said that the $10,000 a year hence is equivalent to only $9,259 today, because by the time we need it, the $9,259 invested at 8 percent will have grown to $10,000.

But suppose that the actual cash wasn't available, all cash resources being tied up in the going business. Assume that one can borrow $10,000 at 5 percent whenever he needs it. In discussing the cost of the new project, one must consider all costs involved, and the 5 percent interest charge would simply become part of each year's cost and would have been figured in as part of the items making up the $10,000 considered necessary for each of the six years in our example. In comparing various projects in order to choose the most attractive ones, one need not go to this refinement, since assuming the "completely liquid" position for all projects puts them on a strictly comparable basis.

Payback

The projected returns of a project should be put on a comparable basis with the net outlays for it by discounting the anticipated future proceeds to arrive at a comparable net present value of those proceeds. Put another way, it is a matter of calculating the amount of money the company would have to invest today at its current earning capacity (in our example this is 8 percent) on capital invested, in order to produce a yield equal to that of the new project in the years ahead. Assume that the hypothetical new project would, as depicted in Table 2, yield a net return of $5,000 in the sixth year, double that in the seventh year, improve that by another 50 percent to $15,000 during the eighth year, and yield $20,000 a year for the next six years. The total projected return is $150,000 but discounted at 8 percent over the period from the seventh year through the fifteenth year this would be equivalent to the returns from a lump sum of $67,043 invested today, returning 8 percent.

The difference between the present value of the $60,000 outlay shown in Table 1 and the present value of the return, $67,043 less $49,926, is the extra yield of the proposed new product program, on a net-present-value basis for comparison with the investment of the $60,000 in the going business or in an investment returning the same 8 percent on capital achieved by the going business. Obviously, this procedure furnishes a way of comparing a proposed new product with any number of alternative proposed programs, all put on the same present value basis.

Table 3(*a*), (*b*), and (*c*) shows a broad range of interest rates and numbers of years for present value of one dollar based on annual compounding.

An alternative discounted cash flow method is also used. Suppose someone had a situation involving, as discussed above, investments of varying amounts over a number of years, bringing in a return in varying amounts spread over other years, and he wished to determine the actual percentage rate of return achieved on the net total investment. He could do this with the aid of present-value tables by comparing all elements involved in the investment with all of the elements involved on the earning side, with the difference in the timing of the money flows again being recognized by the application of a trial discount rate. By trial and error, a rate will eventually

Table 2. Present value of future returns at 8 percent, compounded annually.

End of Year	Projected Return	Discount Factor	Present Value of Net Return
6	$ 5,000	.6302	$ 3,151
7	10,000	.5835	5,835
8	15,000	.5403	8,105
9	20,000	.5002	10,004
10	20,000	.4632	9,264
11	20,000	.4289	8,578
12	20,000	.3971	7,942
13	20,000	.3677	7,354
14	20,000	.3405	6,810
	$150,000		$67,043

A total of $67,043 invested today on an 8 percent return basis would provide a cash flow of $150,000 over the nine years shown under "Projected Return." Comparison of the present value of net return of alternative proposals allows for the effect of the timing factor on future income and considers the earning power of capital invested in the regular business.

Table 3. *Present value of one dollar.*

A

Percent

Year	1	2	3	4	5	6	7	8	9	10
1	0.9901	0.9804	0.9709	0.9615	0.9524	0.9434	0.9346	0.9259	0.9174	0.9091
2	0.9803	0.9612	0.9426	0.9246	0.9070	0.8900	0.8734	0.8573	0.8417	0.8264
3	0.9706	0.9423	0.9151	0.8890	0.8638	0.8396	0.8163	0.7938	0.7722	0.7513
4	0.9610	0.9238	0.8885	0.8548	0.8227	0.7921	0.7629	0.7350	0.7084	0.6830
5	0.9515	0.9057	0.8626	0.8219	0.7835	0.7473	0.7130	0.6806	0.6499	0.6209
6	0.9420	0.8880	0.8375	0.7903	0.7462	0.7050	0.6663	0.6302	0.5963	0.5645
7	0.9327	0.8706	0.8131	0.7599	0.7107	0.6651	0.6227	0.5835	0.5470	0.5132
8	0.9235	0.8535	0.7894	0.7307	0.6768	0.6274	0.5820	0.5403	0.5019	0.4665
9	0.9143	0.8368	0.7664	0.7026	0.6446	0.5919	0.5439	0.5002	0.4604	0.4241
10	0.9053	0.8203	0.7441	0.6756	0.6139	0.5584	0.5083	0.4632	0.4224	0.3855
11	0.8963	0.8043	0.7224	0.6496	0.5847	0.5268	0.4751	0.4289	0.3875	0.3505
12	0.8874	0.7885	0.7014	0.6246	0.5568	0.4970	0.4440	0.3971	0.3555	0.3186
13	0.8787	0.7730	0.6810	0.6006	0.5303	0.4688	0.4150	0.3677	0.3262	0.2987
14	0.8700	0.7579	0.6611	0.5775	0.5051	0.4423	0.3878	0.3405	0.2992	0.2633
15	0.8613	0.7430	0.6419	0.5553	0.4810	0.4173	0.3624	0.3152	0.2745	0.2394
16	0.8528	0.7284	0.6232	0.5339	0.4581	0.3936	0.3387	0.2919	0.2519	0.2176
17	0.8444	0.7142	0.6050	0.5134	0.4363	0.3714	0.3166	0.2703	0.2311	0.1978
18	0.8360	0.7002	0.5874	0.4936	0.4155	0.3503	0.2959	0.2502	0.2120	0.1799
19	0.8277	0.6864	0.5703	0.4746	0.3957	0.3305	0.2765	0.2317	0.1945	0.1635
20	0.8195	0.6730	0.5537	0.4564	0.3769	0.3118	0.2584	0.2145	0.1784	0.1486
21	0.8114	0.6598	0.5375	0.4388	0.3589	0.2942	0.2415	0.1987	0.1637	0.1351
22	0.8034	0.6468	0.5219	0.4220	0.3418	0.2775	0.2257	0.1839	0.1502	0.1228
23	0.7954	0.6342	0.5067	0.4057	0.3256	0.2618	0.2109	0.1703	0.1378	0.1117
24	0.7876	0.6217	0.4919	0.3901	0.3101	0.2470	0.1971	0.1577	0.1264	0.1015
25	0.7798	0.6095	0.4776	0.3751	0.2953	0.2330	0.1842	0.1460	0.1160	0.0923
26	0.7720	0.5976	0.4637	0.3607	0.2812	0.2198	0.1722	0.1352	0.1064	0.0839
27	0.7644	0.5859	0.4502	0.3468	0.2678	0.2074	0.1609	0.1252	0.0976	0.0763
28	0.7568	0.5744	0.4371	0.3335	0.2552	0.1956	0.1504	0.1159	0.0895	0.0693
29	0.7493	0.5631	0.4243	0.3207	0.2429	0.1846	0.1406	0.1073	0.0822	0.0630
30	0.7419	0.5521	0.4120	0.3083	0.2314	0.1741	0.1314	0.0994	0.0754	0.0573

Table 3. Present value of one dollar (continued).

B

Year	Percent									
	11	12	13	14	15	16	17	18	19	20
1	0.9009	0.8929	0.8850	0.8772	0.8696	0.8621	0.8547	0.8475	0.8403	0.8333
2	0.8116	0.7972	0.7831	0.7695	0.7561	0.7432	0.7305	0.7182	0.7062	0.6944
3	0.7312	0.7118	0.6913	0.6750	0.6575	0.6407	0.6244	0.6086	0.5934	0.5787
4	0.6587	0.6355	0.6133	0.5921	0.5718	0.5523	0.5337	0.5158	0.4987	0.4823
5	0.5935	0.5674	0.5428	0.5194	0.4972	0.4761	0.4561	0.4371	0.4190	0.4019
6	0.5346	0.5066	0.4803	0.4556	0.4323	0.4104	0.3898	0.3704	0.3521	0.3349
7	0.4817	0.4523	0.4251	0.3996	0.3759	0.3538	0.3332	0.3139	0.2959	0.2791
8	0.4339	0.4039	0.3762	0.3506	0.3269	0.3050	0.2848	0.2660	0.2487	0.2326
9	0.3909	0.3606	0.3329	0.3075	0.2843	0.2630	0.2434	0.2255	0.2090	0.1938
10	0.3522	0.3220	0.2946	0.2697	0.2472	0.2267	0.2080	0.1911	0.1756	0.1615
11	0.3173	0.2875	0.2607	0.2366	0.2149	0.1954	0.1778	0.1619	0.1476	0.1346
12	0.2858	0.2567	0.2307	0.2076	0.1869	0.1685	0.1520	0.1372	0.1240	0.1122
13	0.2575	0.2292	0.2042	0.1821	0.1625	0.1452	0.1299	0.1163	0.1042	0.0935
14	0.2320	0.2046	0.1807	0.1597	0.1413	0.1252	0.1110	0.0985	0.0876	0.0779
15	0.2090	0.1827	0.1599	0.1401	0.1229	0.1079	0.0949	0.0835	0.0736	0.0649
16	0.1883	0.1631	0.1415	0.1229	0.1069	0.0930	0.0811	0.0708	0.0618	0.0541
17	0.1696	0.1456	0.1252	0.1078	0.0929	0.0802	0.0693	0.0600	0.0520	0.0451
18	0.1528	0.1300	0.1108	0.0946	0.0808	0.0691	0.0592	0.0508	0.0437	0.0376
19	0.1377	0.1161	0.0981	0.0829	0.0703	0.0596	0.0506	0.0431	0.0367	0.0313
20	0.1240	0.1037	0.0868	0.0728	0.0611	0.0514	0.0433	0.0365	0.0308	0.0261
21	0.1117	0.0926	0.0768	0.0638	0.0531	0.0443	0.0370	0.0309	0.0259	0.0217
22	0.1007	0.0826	0.0680	0.0560	0.0462	0.0382	0.0316	0.0262	0.0218	0.0181
23	0.0907	0.0738	0.0601	0.0491	0.0402	0.0329	0.0270	0.0222	0.0183	0.0151
24	0.0817	0.0659	0.0532	0.0431	0.0349	0.0284	0.0231	0.0188	0.0154	0.0126
25	0.0736	0.0588	0.0471	0.0378	0.0304	0.0245	0.0197	0.0160	0.0129	0.0105
26	0.0663	0.0525	0.0417	0.0331	0.0264	0.0211	0.0169	0.0135	0.0109	0.0087
27	0.0597	0.0469	0.0369	0.0291	0.0230	0.0182	0.0144	0.0115	0.0091	0.0073
28	0.0538	0.0419	0.0326	0.0255	0.0200	0.0157	0.0123	0.0097	0.0077	0.0061
29	0.0485	0.0374	0.0289	0.0224	0.0174	0.0135	0.0105	0.0082	0.0064	0.0051
30	0.0437	0.0334	0.0256	0.0196	0.0151	0.0116	0.0090	0.0070	0.0054	0.0042

Table 3. Present value of one dollar (continued).

C

Year	Percent									
	21	22	23	24	25	26	27	28	29	30
1	0.8264	0.8197	0.8130	0.8065	0.8000	0.7937	0.7874	0.7813	0.7752	0.7692
2	0.6830	0.6719	0.6610	0.6504	0.6400	0.6299	0.6200	0.6104	0.6009	0.5917
3	0.5645	0.5507	0.5374	0.5245	0.5120	0.4999	0.4882	0.4768	0.4658	0.4552
4	0.4665	0.4514	0.4369	0.4230	0.4096	0.3968	0.3844	0.3725	0.3611	0.3501
5	0.3855	0.3700	0.3552	0.3411	0.3277	0.3149	0.3027	0.2910	0.2799	0.2693
6	0.3186	0.3033	0.2888	0.2751	0.2621	0.2499	0.2383	0.2274	0.2170	0.2072
7	0.2633	0.2486	0.2348	0.2218	0.2097	0.1983	0.1877	0.1776	0.1682	0.1594
8	0.2176	0.2038	0.1909	0.1789	0.1678	0.1574	0.1478	0.1388	0.1304	0.1226
9	0.1799	0.1670	0.1552	0.1443	0.1342	0.1249	0.1164	0.1084	0.1011	0.0943
10	0.1486	0.1369	0.1262	0.1164	0.1074	0.0992	0.0916	0.0847	0.0784	0.0725
11	0.1228	0.1122	0.1026	0.0938	0.0859	0.0787	0.0721	0.0662	0.0607	0.0558
12	0.1015	0.0920	0.0834	0.0757	0.0687	0.0625	0.0568	0.0517	0.0471	0.0429
13	0.0839	0.0754	0.0678	0.0610	0.0550	0.0496	0.0447	0.0404	0.0365	0.0330
14	0.0693	0.0618	0.0551	0.0492	0.0440	0.0393	0.0352	0.0316	0.0283	0.0253
15	0.0573	0.0507	0.0448	0.0397	0.0352	0.0312	0.0277	0.0247	0.0219	0.0195
16	0.0474	0.0415	0.0364	0.0320	0.0281	0.0248	0.0218	0.0193	0.0170	0.0150
17	0.0391	0.0340	0.0296	0.0258	0.0225	0.0197	0.0172	0.0150	0.0132	0.0116
18	0.0323	0.0279	0.0241	0.0208	0.0180	0.0156	0.0135	0.0118	0.0102	0.0089
19	0.0267	0.0229	0.0196	0.0168	0.0144	0.0124	0.0107	0.0092	0.0079	0.0068
20	0.0221	0.0187	0.0159	0.0135	0.0115	0.0098	0.0084	0.0072	0.0061	0.0053
21	0.0183	0.0154	0.0129	0.0109	0.0092	0.0078	0.0066	0.0056	0.0048	0.0040
22	0.0151	0.0126	0.0105	0.0088	0.0074	0.0062	0.0052	0.0044	0.0037	0.0031
23	0.0125	0.0103	0.0086	0.0071	0.0059	0.0049	0.0041	0.0034	0.0029	0.0024
24	0.0103	0.0085	0.0070	0.0057	0.0047	0.0039	0.0032	0.0027	0.0022	0.0018
25	0.0085	0.0069	0.0057	0.0046	0.0038	0.0031	0.0025	0.0021	0.0017	0.0014
26	0.0070	0.0057	0.0046	0.0037	0.0030	0.0025	0.0020	0.0016	0.0013	0.0011
27	0.0058	0.0047	0.0037	0.0030	0.0024	0.0019	0.0016	0.0013	0.0010	0.0008
28	0.0048	0.0038	0.0030	0.0024	0.0019	0.0015	0.0012	0.0010	0.0008	0.0006
29	0.0040	0.0031	0.0025	0.0020	0.0015	0.0012	0.0010	0.0008	0.0006	0.0005
30	0.0033	0.0026	0.0020	0.0016	0.0012	0.0010	0.0008	0.0006	0.0005	0.0004

be found that makes the present value of the outflows approximately equal to the present value of the inflows—and this is the rate sought. Usually, a satisfactory approximation of this rate can be found in two or three trials.

Here is how it would work in a hypothetical example: If one tries, as a starter, 15 percent, and uses the figures from Table 3 (a), (b), and (c), he will get a present value of outlays of $43,522. By the same method, the present value of the return comes out as $37,567. This first trial showed the proceeds to be less than the outlays—in other words, the projected investment isn't quite as good as 15 percent, and a lesser figure should be tried. (Conversely, had the trial resulted in a figure larger than the outlays, the next trial should have used a larger rate.) Try 12 percent. The present value of outlays comes to $46,048, and the present value of proceeds comes to $49,327. One went too far, so try 13 percent. Now the present value of outlays comes to $45,173, and proceeds to $42,374. Thus the return of the projected new project comes to between 12 and 13 percent—more than a 50 percent higher rate of return than that achieved from the going business.

The discounted cash method reduces projects with varying time factors and returns to a comparable basis. Every other basis of comparison fails to take into account the fact that payback of dollars far in the future is considerably less profitable than payback in the immediate years ahead.

Industry Position

How big a factor in their respective markets will new products become? If the market position of most of the company's products is at a level of, say, 30 percent, and a new product under consideration does not have a reasonable chance of achieving this position in its own market within a five-year period, it may prove troublesome to the sales organization—it may be too sensitive to competitive forces. If a company produces a diversified line of products, the individual market positions of the varied lines may be quite different. Each new product proposal should be related to the most closely associated existing product line in evaluating the relative potential industry position.

Gross Sales Volume

Over the years, company operations become geared to certain sales levels. It isn't easy for a company to suddenly adjust itself to substantially different ones. For example, if the sales volume of existing products is at the $10-million-a-year level, it would be difficult for most product managers to handle a new product where sales are expected to be at a much lower level. Even if the low-volume item showed promise of having a substantially higher profit margin, the low-volume line might not profitably support the kind of services—research, advertising, sales promotion, and distribution—that would be the familiar operating pattern for higher volume products. There are always special circumstances. Profit profiles are developed to highlight out-of-line factors so that they can be recognized and carefully reviewed.

Rate of Sales Growth

How rapidly will the sales volume of the new product grow? An examination of the rate of growth of the products in the present line provides perspective in evaluating new product projections. Before deciding that an idea is not good enough because sales projections do not show a fast enough growth in sales volume, take a look at the company's history. Answer these questions: How many of the company's products met the criteria for growth that are now being applied? In the light of past performance, how realistic are the criteria?

Rate of Profit Growth

As with the rate of sales volume growth, a look at the rate at which the profit position of proposed products will grow is helpful in comparing proposals.

Hits, Aborts, and Rejects

Finally, take a look at the past ten years and tally the score. How many new products have been successes? How many were failures? How many new ideas were turned down when they were first proposed? A look at the record can be quite revealing. New products turned down may have proved profitable for competitors who subsequently developed similar ones. On the other hand, the record may reveal that so few projects were proposed that management did not feel it could afford to turn down any for fear that there would be no new products at all. Proposals should take the past record into consideration and point to steps that can improve the record as the program goes forward.

Only those managers willing to take the time to tackle the exacting task of making meaningful and realistic profitability projections will be in a position to develop significant decision-making information.

part two
Funding and Auditing

7

Funding
Product Development

HOW much should a company spend for product development? Companies that spend too little find themselves in an unfavorable competitive position. Companies that spend too much find themselves in an unfavorable profit position.

The fact that an exact answer can't be given to the question tends to lull some into complacency. They say, "Since no one can tell us how much to spend we might as well go on guessing." This attitude hasn't led to success, and for a good reason: While you can't determine how much should be spent for product development with the precision you might hope for, you can establish some guidelines that help in positioning product-development activities.

Product development includes all those activities essential to finding out what a company needs to strengthen its product portfolio and what opportunities can be exploited. Needs must be determined. Ideas for new products must be collected and evaluated. The best must be turned into technically and economically feasible products. New products must be put into the hands of satisfied customers to prove that the development can be successful on a larger scale. This is the scope of product development.

Any effective thinking about product development must look at product development as a process in which all the supporting roles played by individual functions are subordinated to the overall objective of developing new products, improved products, and products that can be produced at substantially reduced costs.

The answers to the following ten questions help to determine how much a company should spend for product development.

1. What is the average expenditure for product development in our industry? Expenditures of other companies in the same industry are a measure of the competitive effort. The level of competitive effort isn't sufficient by itself, but it does serve as a bench mark.

In using figures for any industry, one must be sufficiently familiar with the industry to understand the extremes that exist there and to know how to position one's own company within the industry. Then, too, accounting practices vary from company to company.

The fact that the use of industry data calls for judgment and experience shouldn't create particularly unusual problems. All decisions are based on the exercise of judgment.

2. How effective are our product development efforts compared with others in our industry? If five companies in a single industry had identical product lines and each was spending 4 percent of its sales dollar for new product development, one company would probably grow in size and profit position beyond the other four because of its more highly developed skill in developing new products.

3. What is the least we could spend for product development and stay in business? Low limits for product development expenditures are established by the cost of those programs which, if eliminated, would result in a loss of competitive position within a short time. Redesign and product improvement programs may fall into this category. Such projects may have a clearly calculable payoff.

4. Can we use the end products of development programs? In every company, upper limits are established by the ability of the company's management to effectively administer the new problems that necessarily accompany any new product. Can it raise new capital? Is additional management time available? Is manufacturing capacity available? Does the sales force know how to handle new items?

5. What are the uncertainties arising in calculating costs of individual new product undertakings? All new-product-development activities involve uncertainties. When a proposed group of projects appears too heavily weighted on the speculative side, it is a good idea to inject projects having a less speculative nature to balance the mix.

The opposite situation deserves careful inspection too. If most of the projects are of such a nature that their outcome seems assured, the company isn't thinking far enough ahead. By the nature of their products, some industries move forward faster than others. In these situations, a company is forced to undertake speculative programs.

6. To what degree have we been successful in putting new prod-

ucts into the hands of satisfied customers? No new-product-development program will be successful until a sufficient number of customers are satisfied to prove out the venture. When some parts of the process aren't being performed effectively, it is better to reduce the number of projects and to concentrate on the successful completion of these before undertaking others.

7. *Does our management understand the concepts and operating fundamentals that lead to growth?* Size isn't the important factor in achieving growth goals. It is know-how. Nor is growth a matter of company size or age. Both small and large companies have expanded and are expanding. Both well-established and recently organized management teams have been successful in planning for growth.

It has been clearly established that successful product development programs are dependent on management groups that understand the concepts and operating fundamentals basic to establishing the targets, timetables, and techniques that lead to growth.

8. *Are we planning for our future?* Some have become so preoccupied with today's business that they have forgotten all about that of the future. Even in some of the newer, currently expanding businesses, stagnation is apparent.

9. *Have broad objectives been established by management to outline the scope of product development activities?* It is difficult to determine how much should be spent for product development if you don't know what you are trying to accomplish.

In most companies, new products are needed—

> To insure that the company will continue to operate in areas of growing business activity and profit potential.
> To make the best possible use of the company's resources, such as raw materials, technical specialties, and management talent.
> To utilize available markets adequately.
> To insure steadily increasing and stable profits.
> To contribute to the corporation's ability to accept social and humanitarian responsibilities.

A management finding that its programs don't include every one of these broad objectives would find it well worthwhile to reexamine its product programs.

10. *Are we allergic to newness?* Most businesses get their start from a single good idea, and thus begin as pioneers—only, in time, to become conservative and thereby to reject the very process of innovation that brought them into existence. It is equally dangerous to swing to the opposite extreme. While most businesses can trace

their start to a single good product idea it doesn't always follow
that it's best to be first every time.

The important thing is to be able to choose the right category—
innovator, leader, follower, laggard—for the right reason at the right
time. Businesses that have achieved successful growth records have
put themselves in a position where they could choose favorably.

Basis for Effective Action

Those in charge of a business know more about their special needs
than anyone else. Because of this, the above ten questions are all
that can ever be offered. Some will make better use of these questions
than others, and here are some of the reasons why.

First, some have learned how to develop data for decision making.
In the long run, it saves time and trouble if the necessary background
information is developed before decisions are made.

Second, others have gotten more mileage out of their technical
resources. For example, if today's supply of scientific and engineering
manpower were effectively utilized, there wouldn't be any talk of
shortages.

Third, some companies make effective use of their full technical
output rather than wasting new-product-development activities. This
is as opposed to companies where good ideas are shelved while management orients itself to the newness of the idea.

Those who have scored outstanding achievement records haven't
done so because the direction to be taken was indicated by a clearly
blazed path and precise formulas for action. Rather, these records
have been achieved by those who knew how to make good use of
these questions. Management did a better overall job of decision making. It made better use of its technical resources. It made better
than average use of the various functions associated with new product
development. The effectiveness of these questions will be multiplied
many times over as companies develop skill in using them.

Planning for the Future

Speculation seems to be an action substitute for many. Too much
talk about an age of technology seems to dull the sense of some
to the need for action to cope with, not so much problems, as opportunities, for every problem also presents an opportunity. Most deci-

sions that must be made in businsss today are either operations-oriented or opportunity-oriented. To cope with today's needs, they must be both.

The greatest rewards are going to those who can turn this new technology into profitable new products. One of the greatest barriers to doing so results from thinking about parts of the process of product development rather than about the total picture. There is a tendency to deal with research in the physical sciences, engineering, the measurement of consumer acceptance, prototype development, customer application, and product pioneering as if they were utterly unrelated. This results in a waste of time and money stemming from a duplication of efforts and a breakdown in communications.

New-product-development operations have presented a confusing pattern. Diffuse terminology and overlapping functions have been responsible. Because of this the various activities that should have multiplied their individual effectiveness have instead canceled out each other's potential effectiveness. The compartmentalizing effect of terminology—terms such as "applications engineering," "research," and the like—has made it difficult to capture the all-important totality of viewpoint and perspective essential to sound decision making.

Profits depend on the total viewpoint. To grow, the company must expand its resources. It must be able to detect and develop new knowledge, commercially feasible products and processes, and profit opportunities. It must do this job continuously with a minimum of time lag and at the lowest possible cost in dollars and management time.

Some look upon the industrial corporation as one in which men, money, materials, machines, and management are turned into products and profits. But this is true only after ideas and information are turned into plans and programs.

The Job Ahead

Product development has the responsibility of executing functions essential in providing the company with products that will insure its profit position in the years ahead. To do this, programs must be put into motion that will (1) develop new knowledge and understanding of phenomena, materials, and the arts that can be used by the corporation; (2) develop technically and economically feasible products and processes that can be used by the corporation and its customers and that can be produced, distributed, installed, maintained, and serviced; and (3) define profit centers as investment opportunities for further expansion of business through development and acquisition.

To accomplish these ends quickly and effectively, all the important functions essential to the achievement of these objectives must be adequately performed and competently coordinated. Functions that growth companies have found important range from business conditions and technological forecasting to new product pioneering.

To accomplish these ends effectively, there must be clear primary responsibility for these functions. Generating new and profitable products, proving that they can be transformed into profit producers, putting them on the market, and finally, turning them into profit producers are functions uniquely interrelated.

Plans and action patterns must be coordinated for a fast-moving, hard-hitting attack. The effective use of ideas, the total utilization of resources, and sound decision making all depend on this coordination.

Levels of expenditure for product development will and must vary from company to company depending on the degree to which product development activities are coordinated. The more efficiency, the less expense.

Product development isn't an easy undertaking but it is an important one to business growth. Any growing and profitable business organization must concern itself not only with its present position in the market but also with its future. It should recognize that it must always combat competition.

Even where product lines are already returning a satisfactory profit, the product development group must give thought to product changes that will be necessary to maintain or improve these profit positions. New needs and new opportunities must be anticipated, and development work must be initiated to meet them.

A Plan of Action

It is time to toughen up management thinking about products for the future, to broaden this thinking, to think in depth as well as breadth, to think in terms of the scope of these activities. And it is time to hold product planning responsible for figuring out what will pay off and when.

To capture a leadership position, inefficiencies and wasted resources must be minimized. Corporations must be structured so as to utilize new developments and to examine each in its own setting, and to capitalize on these new ideas through management methods tailored to take advantage of these new ideas. To achieve this, the horizons of management thinking must be broadened; those activities that create, guide, and coordinate development programs must be given top-level attention; and to foster future growth, management must be assured that properly disciplined minds are searching in the right directions.

Technology is advancing at an alarming rate, creating conditions calling for sweeping reappraisals of management thinking and action patterns. Only by such reappraisals can management turn ideas into dollars at the lowest possible cost.

8

Profit Opportunities in Present Products

SOME of the greatest rewards come from concentrating on existing products. The desire to do something new and different, to diversify, to introduce new products is liable to tempt one to look too far away too soon. The cow grazing in the pasture and hankering for that greener grass on the other side of the fence has her corporation counterpart—the man who is always looking for greener products.

There is nothing wrong in wanting to do something new and different. New products are essential to survival, but the point is not to overlook the profit potential of existing products. Indeed, some of the best opportunities to do something different grow out of working with familiar products and markets.

A well-thought-out development plan starts with the things that management knows best and the markets with which it is familiar. These should be developed to the fullest to provide additional income that can be used for expanding activities into new and different directions—as time, money, and energy become available.

Today's Profit Base: Present Products in Present Markets

A close look at already familiar products and markets before going on to new kinds of activities will reveal things about operations that aren't seen so clearly when working with unfamiliar products in unfamiliar markets. A close look at familiar products will point up weaknesses in research, engineering, manufacturing, sales, finance, and management. While these usually entail criticism where familiar products are concerned, they may well be excused as part of the learning process in undertaking new activities. This is one of the reasons why some managers are eager to continually undertake new projects. These men figure that if they run fast enough with new undertakings, their mistakes aren't so apt to catch up with them. This can prove costly to a company.

It's a good idea to be sure that present products and present markets are being fully developed and supported by the company's present programs. When this isn't true, it is too soon to move forward into new product areas and new markets.

Eight Action Areas

Jumping too far too soon into new product areas may conceal important operating facts that aren't highlighted clearly by new ventures. The sound approach is to start out by focusing attention on the company's present product position. The key question to ask and answer is this: How can the company increase its return on investment from existing products in present markets without product innovation?

Those in the company responsible for developing new products are usually the same people responsible for existing products. Take time to see what steps will help them improve their performance with current products. Capabilities can be developed more readily when working with what is familiar. Then, when new programs get under way, those responsible for them will be able to move forward faster.

To take full advantage of profit opportunities for existing products, it is important to take effective action in a number of areas. A company's products occupy an optimum product posture when they do the jobs customers want done at a price customers are willing to pay and at a cost favorable to the company that supplies the product. To achieve this, it is important that each of eight important action areas be examined. They are manufacturing, packaging, distribution, pricing, selling, installation, utilization, and maintenance and servicing.

Manufacturing
Since a product originates with manufacturing specifications this is a good place to begin. To pinpoint worthwhile areas for examination

some questions can be asked. Any one of these questions could lead to several years' work for those given the specific responsibility for taking the action needed to tap opportunities.

A major question: Can the product line be simplified? Over a period of time new customer needs and new developments are incorporated into existing product lines. Time is not always taken to reexamine product lines to see whether or not refinements should be consolidated. The addition of new features may complicate rather than simplify.

One company started out making a small voltmeter. It had a range of six volts and a circular dial. A second customer came along and asked for this same meter with the same range but with a square face. As a result, an additional meter was added to the line. Still later, a customer came along and wanted a meter with a range of five volts. A third meter was added to the line. This went on until there were over 100 active meter models. Each model had as many as eight functional variations, and each functional variation had dozens of ranges and scale calibrations. A review of customer requirements with an eye toward simplification revealed that upwards of 90 percent of sales requirements could be met by three basic mechanisms.

Simplification paid off for this meter manufacturer in more ways than one. Manufacturing costs were reduced. Distribution centers had fewer models to carry in stock. There were still other advantages, and these will be discussed as part of other action areas. Anything done to take advantage of opportunities lying in a particular action area is usually reflected by benefits in other such areas.

Another major question: Can components be standardized? Designers select components best suited for specific functions in particular products. This results in optimum design for that particular product. As product lines grow in size and complexity, many components perform the same function in different products but differ in their individual design specifications. This introduces new problems that outweigh the advantages gained from initial optimum-design specifications.

In one case a line of refrigerators used 14 different sizes of screws and types of screws to fasten the refrigerator door hinge. Each size was just right for a particular weight door and a particular type of hinge. An overall review of the specifications indicated that the screw used for the hinge on the refrigerator having the heaviest door could be adapted to all of the models by using fewer units of the stronger screw for the lighter weight doors, and that this could be done without increasing the total cost for any one model in the line. At the same time, other economies were affected. Manufacturing and service stocks were reduced substantially. In another case, 12 different chemical compounds used for cleaning metals in 12 different divisions of a multidivisional company were reduced to a single cleaning compound at a considerable cost savings.

A value analysis of present products always pays off in both an increased return on investment and a better understanding of the company's product. Reappraisals of product lines with a view toward simplification and standardization should be a continuing practice rather than an intermittent act. Product lines are always responding to new developments and new customer requirements. The drift, however, is always in the direction of increased complexity. Reappraisals in the manufacturing action area help counteract complexity.

Packaging

Can functional features be incorporated in packaging? Some still think of packages as just the wrapping on a product, but packaging incorporates important functional features. One of the most important is to protect a product from damage during shipping. And packaging plays other important roles.

The design of the package can provide for an inventory of the components that must be delivered to the customer. For example, one manufacturer packages an electronic unit in a transparent plastic block that has a cavity in the block for each of the component parts of the electronic unit. Labeling on the clear plastic package clearly identifies each of the components. In the final inspection process before shipping, an empty cavity will call the inspector's attention to a missing part. At the same time, when the customer receives the unit he is able to identify each of the parts before unpacking them and is less likely to discard some of the component parts with the packing material. In this particular unit, assembly of the components is facilitated because the parts are segregated for easy identification when the user studies the instruction manual.

One manufacturer of a mechanical assembly puts the unit with its mounting bracket and mounting screws in a sealed can in order to eliminate loss of the parts from the package on the retail display shelf. The package is also used to facilitate the shelving of an irregularly shaped object.

One of the very important roles that the package can play is selling the features of the product itself as well as keeping the company's name before potential customers. Manufacturers of consumer products have long recognized the value of the package as a selling tool. Manufacturers of technical products, mechanical goods, electrical units, and chemicals, are making increasing use of the package to tell a story to potential users as well as to those who have already purchased the product. Such information can be important—as in making sure that the customer is properly acquainted with the proper use of the product before he opens the package.

Distribution

Can the product be designed so as to expedite shipping and shelving? One manufacturer of instruments made mechanical changes in the design that resulted in instruments relatively damage-proof in shipping. Earlier, large masses of metal were supported by pinions. Careful handling had been required to avoid excessive breakage during shipment. Other changes in the basic design of the instrument resulted in a device that had square contour rather than cylindrical contour. This reduced damage while instruments were on the shelf in stockrooms.

Can the shelf life be increased? Many products are used intermittently. Sometimes a year may go by before a product is taken off a distributor's shelf and sold to a customer. The customer may put the product away for long periods between use. Manufacturers of fire extinguishers are well aware that shelf life is an important factor in performance. Here is a product that every customer hopes will have long periods of inactivity, but yet must perform without any loss of effectiveness when it's called on.

Management frequently fails to recognize that long shelf life is a determinant of success with most products. For example, in one case a battery-operated dictating unit is used after long periods of inactivity. If the batteries in such a unit have lost their effectiveness, or even worse, have corroded and damaged the equipment, it will be difficult to sell this equipment on a repeat basis. The company that manufactures dictating equipment incorporating long-shelf-life features will get the repeat order.

Or take the case of photographic film. All such film passes through a distributor and dealer before it reaches the more or less temporary stock of an amateur or professional consumer. During this time, the manufacturer loses control of his product and the product may be subjected to overly long periods of storage, changes of temperature, and other conditions that may damage or reduce its quality. It may be difficult to do anything about all these factors, yet any steps that can be taken to increase the shelf life of the product will improve its performance and increase customer satisfaction.

In looking for profit opportunities in existing products, distribution should be given careful attention. No two products have the same kinds of distribution requirements. Each of the facets of distributing a particular product should be carefully examined to find out what opportunities exist to put a better product in the hands of its customer in a less costly and less time-consuming way.

Pricing

Should the product be re-priced for sales–profit-position opportunities? Profit opportunities may be lost because products are priced either too high or too low to take advantage of existing market opportunities. The relationship between price and markets is not as well understood as it should be by those responsible for product programs.

Too many still associate price with cost. Obviously, no company can afford to sell a product below its cost for too long a time or it will be out of business. The difference between the price the customer pays for the product and the cost to the manufacturer represents the product's profit.

From a practical standpoint, however, it's the price of a product that is a determinant of the cost, rather than the cost that is a determinant of the price. Contradictory as this may seem, in the case of most products it's the price of the product that determines sales volume, and sales volume is the biggest single determinant of the cost of most products.

While generally what is wanted is high volume to develop a low selling price, this is not always the case. For example, the creator of a high-fashion item such as an exclusive evening gown may price on the basis of a very high dollar figure with the objective of reducing sales volume to a single sale.

In sharp contrast, the firm that may copy this design later will apply an entirely different price policy to an almost identical item. The evening gown will be priced at the lowest possible figure consistent with volume production.

While this pricing relationship is well understood in the apparel trades these same relationships should be considered with respect to other products. For example, the Model T Ford was priced for mass ownership. Eastman priced the Kodak for sales in the mass markets. The Cadillac is of course priced for prestige sales as is the Leica camera.

Some years ago, at a time when a fountain pen or a good mechanical pencil in the better quality group sold for $5, the Reynolds ballpoint pen was introduced at a price in excess of $15 although it cost only a few cents to produce. Few products have ever achieved the phenomenal market reception that accompanied its introduction. It raises some interesting questions. Would this product have been accorded the same distinction had it been priced at $1?

While price must cover costs, there is an optimum price for every product. When one talks about the utility value of a product to a customer, it's important to remember that price may have a utility in the form of prestige.

To cite another product example familiar to almost everyone, one of the best mechanical pencils on the market is sold in three different price brackets, depending on the amount of gold in the pencil's outer shell. In each of the three classes of outer shell, the quality is more than adequate for a lifetime of use, since each of the three shells is gold-filled rather than gold-plated. From a utility standpoint, the lowest priced item represents the best wear resistance of the three gold alloys used. However, from a practical standpoint, each of the three pencils fills a particular market that would not be adequately served by the other two. Unquestionably, price has a utility value to the customer; that value shouldn't be overlooked by those responsible for pricing products.

Selling

Are sales calls carefully prepared? Those who know how to sell know that the sales call starts a long way away from the customer. The proper starting point for the sales call is the preparation that builds the background and strategy that always form the basis for the effective sales presentation. Yet how often this is overlooked.

Many products are complex and require careful study by the salesman if he is to answer competently the questions his customers ask. Altogether too often the answer to a single question may be the deciding factor that leads the customer to buy the product. Yet with some of the simplest products the salesman appears to be the least well-informed. There are department store clerks who aren't aware of the size range of merchandise on display in their department. As a result they turn sales away when items are available. A customer who wanted to buy a dress shirt in a particular size was told by a clerk in one store that the manufacturer did not make this particular size in the style he wanted. A clerk in a second department store checked the manufacturer's catalog and made a sale.

Preparation for the sale must go beyond knowledge of the item and the various catalog designations. It requires knowledge of the features that distinguish it from the competition's product. Yet salesmen aren't always able to explain to a customer why a particular product is better than another. Sometimes the salesman sees only the external features. For example, a potential customer inquiring about an electric watch asked what features made it a better watch, and was told by one salesman that it was better simply because the customer wouldn't have to wind it. A second salesman, however, explained that it was a better timekeeper because an electric watch was always fully wound. The second salesman sold the product. In another case, two competitive products had identical performance characteristics, but one salesman was aware that one of the two competitive brands was more uniform with respect to quality.

It's a good idea to ask a lot of questions about selling practices in looking for profit opportunities in existing products. Not only is the salesman's preparation for the sale important, not only is it important to make sure that all available sales aids are fully used, but it is important to make sure that the company is taking full advantage of the salesman's contact with the customer. Here, the salesman has an opportunity to learn about things the customer needs, the way products are performing, and other things important to the company. All of these can lead to additional profits.

Installation

Where products require installation, the installation itself may offer profit opportunities. Proper installation is essential to the successful operation and performance of a product with special requirements.

Can the installation time be reduced? A time savings here is a direct cost savings. And for the customer who is anxious to get the product into use, a time savings represents not only a cost factor but also a goodwill factor. The ways installation time can be reduced are not limited to just working faster. It's a problem for designers, manufacturers, distribution people, marketing and sales personnel, and others. For example, if the product must be mounted on a special foundation because of vibration, can vibration be eliminated by a redesign? If the product operates on 220 volts and requires special wiring, can it be redesigned to operate on 110 volts? Questions like these can lead to steps that cut installation time.

Utilization

Does the product do the job the way the customer wants it done? The customer is the final judge of product performance. When the customer isn't satisfied, a product has failed at its most critical point. Engineers and others often try to substitute their own judgment of what the customer needs for what the customer really wants. The better technical design of an automobile may sacrifice rapid acceleration for longer engine life, yet the model with fast pickup is the one that sells. The high-fidelity system that's designed to satisfy the audio expert may remain on the shelf while a system that breaks windows with the high notes sells.

Do the instructions tell the customer how to operate his product? Not always! There are too many customers who don't know what all of the buttons are for, or who don't know how to adjust the product for best performance. Poorly written instruction books may be the culprit. Tell the customer how it works in clear, readable language.

Maintenance and Servicing

Few products perform satisfactorily without periodic maintenance and service. With many products it's difficult to distinguish between the two. Normally, though, maintenance activities are those that keep a product in top operating condition—as, for example, oiling the bearing keeps it in running order—while service functions are those that have to do with fixing products—when the bearing wears out it must be replaced.

It is impossible to discuss maintenance activities without also discussing service functions. Poor maintenance makes frequent servicing necessary. Poor servicing increases maintenance costs.

Can repairs be simplified? Customers will keep products in better working order when they themselves can make minor adjustments and repairs. One of the reasons why simple adjustments and repairs are often neglected is the need for special tools. Even the common screwdriver can be a special tool. When the screw that holds the crank arm on the office pencil sharpener becomes loose and no one has a screwdriver, the arm falls off and the manufacturer is blamed for a poor product. The manufacturer of pencil sharpeners who designs his product so that all repairs can be made by using a dime instead of a screwdriver has simplified minor repairs.

Can maintenance be eliminated? New developments in component parts can be used to eliminate maintenance and reduce down time. So-called oilless bearings give the customer a lifetime of service and satisfaction. Self-setting circuit breakers eliminate the need to replace a blown fuse.

Can servicing be simplified? Some portable dictating machines use special batteries available only from the manufacturer. Others use readily available flashlight batteries. It's easy to decide which dictating machine is the least likely to create battery problems for the customer.

Can service be made more readily available? Customers don't like to have to search out service facilities. In fact, many products are bought simply because buyers know they don't have to worry about repairs. When a company can't provide its own service facilities on a broad geographic basis, it should consider teaming up with some other manufacturer whose service facilities do have good geographic distribution.

Can it be made more rugged? "Treat it as you would a fine watch" is an expression one doesn't hear anymore. The finest watches are shockproof, dustproof, waterproof, and rustproof—and literally foolproof, too, for they even wind themselves. There are things that can be done, however, to make other products more rugged—more foolproof. If the product uses radio tubes, transistors would make it more resistant to abuse. If it uses film, the film can be put in a cartridge so that the customer won't have to fuss with the mechanism, possibly stripping gears and letting dust in. These things, though, have been done; think of something new.

These are just a few questions that have been asked and answered in exploiting profit opportunities in existing products. By eliminating, reducing, or simplifying product maintenance and servicing, costs are reduced for the manufacturer, distributor, dealer, service organization, and, most importantly, the customer. Product life is prolonged and everyone is that much closer to being satisfied.

The Profit Potential of Present Products

Almost everyone has used some product only to discover shortcomings and failings. The screws were in the wrong place, or it was almost impossible to install, or parts weren't available. When this happens, it means that those responsible for the product have failed to do all the things that should have been done. This is because too many managers overlook opportunities to improve existing products. Familiarity may not lead to contempt, but it often leads to neglect—neglect of opportunities to do what could be done.

Times change. Technological advances create new ways of doing things and new materials that can be used to do things better than they have been done before. Customer needs change, too. Both technology and changing customer requirements create profit opportunities in existing products for those willing to ask questions on a continuing basis and to act in these eight action areas.

9

The Protectable Part
of Proprietary Product
and Process Positions

THEFTS of valuable trade secrets, which take place much too often, remind those responsible for new product programs that stolen trade secrets prove costly to a company. When secrets are stolen, those responsible for new products ring the burglar alarm but sometimes fail to lock the barn door.

Today there is too much worry about theft of trade secrets and too little action taken to hold on to them. In fact, companies are giving trade secrets away faster than they are being stolen. The cause of this is clear—the real nature of trade secrets isn't understood.

Those responsible for new product programs are relatively well-informed about patents but they aren't familiar with the real nature of trade secrets or their significance to their company's profit position. Most managers of technical programs and new product development admit that they aren't doing all that could be done. They'll even admit that they aren't sure that they know what a trade secret is, let alone how trade secrets should be protected.

Why Is the Problem So Serious Today?

More and more is heard about trade secrets today because new product technology is assuming an increasingly important role in determining the company's profit picture. Trade secrets go hand in hand with the development and utilization of new technology by a corporation. This ties trade secrets to profit positions.

The loss of a trade secret today shows up in tomorrow's profit column. When this happens those responsible for new products are asked how and why trade secrets were revealed to competitors. Twenty years ago, even ten years ago, the trade secret–profit position relationship wasn't as acute as it is now. Today, the situation is serious. As a company's investment in new know-how spirals upward, those responsible for technical programs and new product development must become better informed about trade secrets so they can provide adequate protection for them.

Who Does What?

Accompanying all new-product and new-process development is an accumulation of supporting data that is an extremely valuable company asset. A company's legal department or outside counsel can help protect a company's trade secrets in a competent manner provided that adequate working relationships are maintained between the product department and the legal department. It's the responsibility of the lawyer to know the law and to know how to guide the company's affairs to best advantage within the legal framework.

Yet while lawyers know the law, they aren't authorities in the technical, marketing, and financial fields unless they have had the proper training and experience. Only a few lawyers qualify as competent counselors in any field other than the law. Ordinarily, when the work of lawyers extends beyond their specialty, lawyers must themselves seek competent counsel. It's the responsibility of the scientists and engineers to develop the new products and processes that can be effectively used by the company and its customers. The technical expert and the lawyer must work together and come to a mutual understanding about the kind of information each needs from the other if he is to do his job most effectively in protecting his company's interests. Trade secrets are one such interest.

It would be hard to find a product developer in a responsible management position who isn't conscious of the importance of working closely with the corporation's legal department in acquiring significant patent positions. Yet while product managers and developers are conscious of the importance of patents, they aren't as aware of the importance of trade secrets—even though a trade secret may be more important to a company than a patent.

Are Trade Secrets Recognized?

The starting point in protecting trade secrets is to size up a company's proprietary position with respect to know-how, processes, information, and ideas. Product managers tend to be patent-oriented: They think that something that can't be patented can't be protected. The written record of business experience reveals that a patent may afford the poorest kind of protection. A patent is good for only 17 years; trade secrets have survived longer. Patent protection is limited to novelty and invention; trade secrets afford broader protection.

The formula for Listerine antiseptic wasn't disclosed for 50 years; a patent would have provided protection for only 17 of those 50 years. Coca-Cola's flavor was long a trade secret, a secret that was kept for over 75 years. These are examples of familiar consumer items. Commercial and industrial products have been protected by trade secrets for even longer periods; one metallurgical secret has already been kept for over 300 years!

No one really knows how long trade secrets can survive. The only limit is the ability of a company to keep its secret. Frequently, those who have trade secrets don't even acknowledge their existence, and thus it's impossible to measure the magnitude of the total stake corporations have in them. One usually only knows about trade secrets that have been disclosed inadvertently. This is the basis of the picture of the role trade secrets have played in the success of products and processes.

Those responsible for new product programs must recognize the kinds of things protectable as trade secrets and follow through to give the company the best competitive advantage. What should be protected will vary from company to company depending on the different types of activities carried on by each company, its end products, and the state of the art in its particular industry. The kinds of information are varied but there are some identifying characteristics that will prove helpful.

What Is the Makeup of Trade Secrets?

A company's trade secrets may be in the form of know-how, processes, information, or ideas. Each of these categories is important because the protectable part may lie in any one or all of these areas.

Know-how

A corporation's know-how is all of the knowledge tied to the use of a new invention. All the knowledge of research workers, engineers, product development people, pilot production operators, and those who develop markets for new products and get new products into the hands of customers is part of a company's proprietary position in a product or process; it's valuable know-how. Two companies may be trying to achieve the same goal. The one that develops a workable way owns valuable know-how that can be protected.

Engineering designs, specifications, lists of suppliers, names of potential customers, financial facts, cost data, and information on manufacturing techniques are things that can be protected as know-how. Knowledge about ways to avoid mistakes may be a valuable trade secret, too.

Processes

Production processes represent a sizable investment of technical time and money. As a result of this investment, a company may be able to produce a better product in a shorter time and at a lower cost than its competitors. In order for a company to carry on its activities, employees must be taken into the company's confidence and given access to this very valuable kind of information.

It's important to identify the kinds of processing information that should enjoy secrecy. Proprietary positions in a secret process or formula can only be maintained under circumstances where this kind of information is imparted to others in confidence. Tell the trade and you lose your proprietary rights.

Relative secrecy depends on what's known in the industry. Process information isn't secret information if it's known to those who want to know it, and know it as a matter of general information. It isn't how many know a secret that's important, but how many know of those who want to know it that determines the degree of secrecy.

Secrets that can't be obtained by examining a product or that a person familiar with the state of the art can't search out put a company in a proprietary position even when novelty and invention aren't involved. For example, protection has been provided a process where one part of the process could be established by examining the product that was on the market, where another part of the process made use of equipment familiar in the industry, where still other parts could be identified as prior practices in the industry, and where one of the components of the equipment used in part of the process was commercially available and could be found in the manufacturer's catalog. And that was only part of it. One of the components was identified in patents, one of the components had been disclosed in a trade magazine, competitors engaged in the manufacture of similar processes had discovered and used parts of the process, portions of the process were described in patents that had expired, and certain parts of the process had been revealed in earlier litigation. Notwithstanding all of this, the process was protected.

Information

Information that can be a valuable trade secret is something anyone could acquire by independent effort rather than by disclosure from someone else. The effective cost of independent research over disclosure would be reflected in a time cost, a money cost, and a cost of uncertainty about the completeness and correctness of the information.

The kind of business information that can be considered a trade secret includes information about a wide range of things such as the status of pending patent applications, the fact that applications may not have been filed, information and negotiations for background patents, technical information on patent applications, technical details of particular systems, the details of financing a new venture or a list of prospective customers.

Ideas

Know-how, processes, and information owned by a company depend for protection on the relative secrecy of the subject matter. Ideas that are to be disclosed on a confidential basis must be concrete rather than abstract. Concrete ideas can be protected on the implied contractual basis inherent in a confidential relationship. Abstract ideas must be protected by express contracts where someone agrees to do something, such as paying for an idea or suggestion.

To be concrete, an idea must be in some sense "worked out." One must develop his own method for using an idea to accomplish a definite result because an idea is capable of being developed and used in so many ways other than those that might be in the mind of the person who first had the idea. Concreteness means that an idea must be spelled out in workable detail, but not necessarily physically created. When a proposed idea presents major problems for others to solve, it is not a concrete idea. However, when problems are minor—the kind that are usually solved by technicians—ideas are in a different category; they are concrete.

How Do You Focus In on Trade Secrets?

Those responsible for product programs need guidelines that can be used to help them protect valuable trade secrets. Some important tests of worthwhile secrets can be highlighted. The relative importance of these tests depends on the situation. Tests of trade secrets that product managers and engineers should keep in mind are these.

Trade secrets must be identifiable. The subject matter must be specific rather than vague. Isolate it and describe it to give it the dimensions of an identifiable trade secret. It's hard to protect something when you don't know what you're trying to protect.

Trade secrets must be secret. Products or processes thoroughly familiar to others in the industry aren't trade secrets, but parts of such products or processes may be known without disclosure of a trade secret. As long as no one knows everything, a company can have a trade secret.

Trade secrets must be confidential. Secret information should be made known only to those whose need to know can be established. The extent to which trade secrets are known to employees determines the extent to which secrets are really secrets. A test of secrecy is secrecy itself.

Trade secrets must be guarded. Steps must be taken to protect secrecy. Information can be kept secret only if an effort is made to guard it. If one isn't making an effort to guard information, it may be difficult to prove to others that the company considered the information secret.

Trade secrets must be valuable. Trade secrets are the kinds of things that have a present potential value somewhere, somehow, to the company. If something doesn't have any value to the company why worry? What's there to lose?

Trade secrets must be a result of effort. The things that have cost the company time, money, and effort to develop are things that should be protected as trade secrets when possible. No company wants to give competitors data developed as a result of its own efforts.

Trade secrets must be difficult to duplicate. Information must be of the sort that others would find difficult to duplicate or acquire; something that's easy for competitors to come up with if they wanted it isn't worth much to anyone. However, as the difficulty of acquiring or duplicating certain information becomes greater, the significance of that information to the company as a potential trade secret increases proportionately.

If those responsible for the development of new products keep in mind these seven tests of trade secrets they should find it easier to detect the kinds of information that should be protected. Circumstances will determine their relative importance in any given situation, but these seven tests are good guides for product managers and engineers.

Why Not Apply for a Patent?

In any action having to do with trade secrets, this question should always be asked: "If something is worthwhile, why not apply for a patent?" A great many factors must be weighed in answering it. Several of the most important considerations follow.

Many trade secrets are simply unpatentable. To pass the test of patentability an idea must contain novelty and inventiveness. Trade secrets are much broader in scope.

Even where something is patentable it may be worth more as a trade secret than as a patent. A patent is good for only 17 years; a trade secret has an indefinite lifetime. A patent tells the public about an idea and explains it in workable detail. You tell the world but get protection only in those countries where you apply for specific patents and undertake the responsibility of enforcing and policing your patent's rights. Competitors are given the incentive and the information to work around one's patent, departing from it just sufficiently to defeat one's patent protection.

The difficulty of policing and defending patents is sizable. In many cases it's almost impossible to learn from a finished product whether or not its manufacturer has infringed a process patent. Few manufacturers will allow access to manufacturing facilities for the purpose of checking on possible patent infringement. Even armed with information about the patent infringement, the odds seem to be against a company when it goes into court for the purpose of establishing such infringement.

Must Employees Be Bound by Contractual Agreements?

An employee having access to trade secrets or other confidential information in the course of employment is under an implied obligation not to use this information for his own benefit or that of a rival when he leaves the company. This implied relationship of confidence between an employee and an employer exists independently of an express employment contract covering confidence.

These restrictions imposed on employees have been enforced where an employee has set up an independent business of a nature similar to his former employer's business and used the trade secrets of his employer. It's best to call the company's position with respect to proprietary information to the attention of employees in the form of a carefully worded employee agreement. Under such circumstances both the employer and the employee have a clear understanding of the specific things to which they have agreed in the event of termination of employment. Agreements also call the attention of each employee to the fact that a defection by a fellow employee can affect the company's future as well as the individual's job security.

Underlying any kind of agreement between an employer and an employee must be recognition of the fact that an employer cannot prevent his employees from using the skill, knowledge, and experience they have acquired in the course of their work. There are certain things an employee will acquire because these things are common in the industry and would have been acquired whether the employee worked for his firm or a competitor.

This matter of an employee agreement must be given careful consideration. Otherwise, a restrictive agreement designed to protect confidential information may fail at this point. Companies may further protect themselves by agreeing to make payments to a former employee for a period of time after his termination in the event that he is unable to obtain employment as a result of a restrictive agreement in his employment contract.

How Do You Avoid Giving Trade Secrets Away?

In avoiding a giveaway program for trade secrets, some guidelines will prove helpful. While it is impossible to pinpoint every consideration that should be reviewed to cover all possible circumstances, these six steps should prove useful:

1. *Know the nature of your trade secrets;* identify them. Don't discover your trade secrets on the basis of what someone thought worthwhile enough to steal. Don't let someone else prove he is smart enough to recognize your trade secret first. If he does, he will also be smart enough to put up some pretty stiff opposition.

2. *Disclose trade secrets on a need-to-know basis* and no other, and to individuals who have signed a written employee agreement. Sign up those who are not employed by the company, too, if they must know about trade secrets. Fit the agreement you use to the situation you face.

3. *Don't disclose more parts of a trade secret* than will be required by the job to be done.

4. *Restrict plant tours.* Don't reveal trade secrets to visitors, friends, and stockholders. There are enough other things of interest to show them.

5. *Don't let your technical and nontechnical people talk trade secrets away* or "write" them off to build their own prestige. Be sure to censor talks with a sharp pencil; say "no" when in doubt. Be sure you know how, why, when, and where talks or articles benefit the company; these may just represent one more waste of time and money from a profit position as well as a major leakage of trade secrets.

6. *Have a written agreement* that calls attention to the role trade secrets play in protecting everyone's interests in the company and its profits, their job and their future.

How Does a Company Protect Itself from Unsolicited Disclosure?

The problem of avoiding unsolicited disclosure of the trade secrets of others is part of the overall picture, too. Every company has an implied obligation to conduct its own business so as not to unnecessarily or unfairly injure that of another company. One who obtains a disclosure by fraudulent action of course runs the risk of paying a severe penalty. On the other hand, if a company learns the trade secret of another by mistake it may be liable to the other if it knew that the information was a trade secret disclosed by mistake. The best course of action is to make it clearly understood that one cannot consider any idea or invention, unless a patent application has been filed by its originator.

How Does a Company Protect Its Proprietary Position?

If those responsible for new product programs recognize that accompanying all new product and new process development is an accumulation of supporting data extremely important to a company and if they identify the specific data that is really valuable to the company, they will be well on their way toward helping to protect the company's proprietary position. A company's legal department and outside counsel can help protect the company's trade secrets in a competent manner provided that adequate working relationships are maintained between the product people and the legal people.

Management groups that have plans for the future must have the assurance that today's profit base is protected. Without this protection, plans for the future can't unfold. Protecting proprietary positions also protects the profits on which future business growth is based.

10

Auditing
Product Programs

IS each of the company's products really making money? Are any approaching obsolescence? How many new product ideas are in the mill? Will the new products fit into overall future plans?

Answers to such questions clear the way for intelligent decision—and effective action. They can be obtained only through continuous appraisal of the product portfolio.

It can't be emphasized often enough—the only reason for being in business is to produce products at a profit. The products on which profits are based deserve more attention than they usually receive. Prosperity and growth are the results of soundly planned product portfolios reflecting a smooth flow of products throughout the various phases of creating, producing, and distributing.

It isn't enough to create products. These individual products must fit into product portfolios. These portfolios, in turn, must be reexamined to evaluate the effect of new products on older products and to sense both needs and opportunities.

For effective appraisal of product portfolios, the whole product spectrum must be scrutinized, from the creation of product ideas to the final sale. Increasing technological complexity and the increasing intensity of competition involving industrial products demand that those responsible for the development of new products also accept the responsibility for assuring balanced portfolios.

Where is the starting point? The admission by one manager that he had been under severe criticism for concentrating on products that were troublemakers rather than those that were profit producers reflects the misplaced emphasis frequently encountered. In filling the role of troubleshooter, managers can and should provide the type of leadership and direction to product programming that prevent problems from arising by eliminating them at their source.

Errors of judgment are too common. The only sure way to know where to concentrate effort is through continuing analysis of the company's product portfolio.

Developing a Plan of Attack

The basic ingredient of success in any undertaking is a well-organized plan of attack. To determine the strong and weak points in different product lines, it is necessary to separately examine the performance of individual product lines.

A company's image in the eyes of its customers is usually established on a product-line basis. The multiple-plant manufacturer in the electrical industry may be a producer of household appliances to one group of customers and a producer of construction materials to another. The large machinery company, similarly, may be a supplier of automatic lathes to one and textile machines to another. To strengthen product programs the customer-centered product line is the place to start.

Balancing a Product Line

Favorable or unfavorable returns from a product line over any significant span of time reflects the degree of balance achieved in the portfolio of products identified as the product line. At a given time, a low return on invested capital in a particular product line may be due to the introduction of new products to strengthen the line. Another cause of poor returns may be the fact that one or more products have become obsolete but are being carried until replacements can be generated. These and other circumstances may justify a low return on invested capital. Unusually high returns are attributable to equally transitory factors.

To analyze individual product lines, you should see that each product in production, as well as those in the development and pre-development phases, is positioned with respect both to its own individual life cycle and the basic objectives of the product offerings of the business. The composite picture reveals the degree to which the company is meeting objectives and protecting future earnings by providing for a continuing supply of new products to replace those becoming obsolete. It also reveals the degree to which a company is taking full advantage of opportunities to introduce lower-cost products and restyled items, as well as those designed for improved performance, new markets, and new uses.

Synchronizing Product Efforts

In the life cycle of a product, ten distinct phases are recognizable. These include five pre-market categories—prospective, speculative, potentially profitable, scheduled, developmental—and five in-market categories—competitive, obsolescent, dropout, introductory, growth.

One of the important indicators of a soundly planned program is the presence of at least several products in each phase. The fundamental importance of each of these individual phases to overall profits will be reviewed, starting first with the competitive phase of their life cycle.

Competitive Phase

In most companies it would be expected that the bulk of the product effort would be classified as competitive. Products would be well-established in markets that had proved attractive. As a consequence of these attractive markets, others in the industry would have similar product offerings.

Prices and profits would normally have reached rather well-defined upper limits as the opportunity for market exploitation was curtailed and opportunities to reduce costs through greater volume became more difficult. The competitive phase of a product's life would normally reflect a growth of volume and profits followed by a leveling off and some mild decline.

Obsolescent Phase

Products should be regarded as having passed from the competitive phase of their life cycle into the obsolescent phase when a pronounced downward trend in sales volume is clearly indicated. For as long a period as steps can be taken to prolong the time before this downward trend becomes established, products should be regarded as competitive. As soon as it becomes evident that all the available resources that can be used to maintain healthy sales are exhausted, it should be recognized that the forces of obsolescence have taken control of the situation.

Classification of a product as obsolescent does not imply that there are no further profit opportunities in the product offering. Profitable sales may be enjoyed for a considerable period of time after a product is so classified.

Steps should be taken to project the probable time at which individual products will become unprofitable. Dropping products from the line calls for careful planning. Dropping products merely because they are unprofitable may have far-reaching effects on the sale of other products. Even though they are unprofitable, certain items, because they round out the total product line, should be carried until replacement items can be introduced.

Dropout Phase

Classification in the dropout phase serves as a reminder to management that specific products have been assigned scheduled dates on which they are to be dropped from the line. In some instances, the date may be set 30 or 60 days ahead; in others the dropout date may be set months ahead. The selling organization must prepare dealers and distributors for the discontinuance of these items. At the same time, this classification calls to the attention of those responsible for the product portfolio the necessity of scheduling replacement items that should be available prior to the scheduled dropout dates.

Introductory Phase

In another phase of the product life cycle are those new products being placed on the market for the first time. These products should be classified as introductory. Here it is important to note not only the products themselves but specific reasons why these new products are being introduced. Generally speaking, new products are introduced into the line to increase sales and profits and to replace products that are dropping out of the product portfolio.

Five major competitive opportunities should be capitalized on by new product offerings. Soundly planned programs should reflect new product offerings falling into each of the following categories:

1. *Lower cost.* Any redesign resulting in a substantial cost reduction should be regarded as an important new product offering. Lower cost usually changes the profit position of the product either as a

result of increased margin per unit of sales or as a result of potentially greater sales volume at the lower selling price.

2. *Restyling.* The redesign of a product, resulting in greater sales appeal and added consumer acceptance, is a major competitive opportunity for the introduction of a new product.

3. *Improved performance.* Reengineering existing products for improved performance offers a fertile and commonly exploited area of competitive opportunity.

4. *New markets.* Exploiting new markets may be accomplished either by extending existing products into new areas or by introducing radically new products.

5. *New uses.* Another major competitive opportunity is that of adapting products to new uses. These new uses may represent an extension of the area of application of present products or they may represent a radical departure from existing products.

These five major competitive opportunities overlap and any consideration of the category of new uses provides an example of such overlapping. But this is not a serious limitation on the system of classification because it forces product planners to use their imagination and the result can only be for the good. The category of new uses directs attention specifically to capitalizing on opportunities to extend the usefulness of present products.

Many products can be used for more than one purpose. Exploitation of these new uses increases sales. For example, the tongue depressor the physician uses in throat examinations can also be effectively used to mark the location of plants in the garden. Such extremes of end use apply with many products. To find these new uses, product planners must exercise both ingenuity and imagination.

These five major competitive opportunities have been explored in some detail because they are important not only in planning new products but in auditing product programs once they are under way. The five categories stimulate thinking in the planning stage by calling attention to the full spectrum of opportunities. Beyond this they provide a reference framework for measuring the effectiveness of product offerings in accomplishing these specific end purposes.

Growth Phase

As soon as a product has proved its ability to capture market acceptance and to increase sales volume, it should be classified in the growth phase. This is another reason why the introductory phase will seldom if ever show a net profit.

Dividing Line

Up to this point, only those phases in the product cycle where products are offered for sale have been considered. In these five categories, in-market items in the product portfolio are classified.

The second group, pre-market items, is less tangible. Nevertheless, these items are equally important considered from the long-range position of the company.

Prospective Phase

Each proposal for a new product remains in the prospective phase until it can be appraised, helping to form a stockpile of ideas that should be part of a continuing process of finding, screening, and appraising. Unless the hopper of new ideas is full at all times, the screening and appraising function grinds to a halt for lack of raw material. Once halted, this operation is hard to get going again. A healthy stockpile of unappraised ideas is a positive sign of a vigorous product development program.

Prospective product proposals should be found classified under each of the five major competitive opportunities previously discussed. Unfilled classifications on the chart may reveal a lack of vigorous action on the part of those who hold the responsibility for developing ideas for new products.

Speculative Phase

In the process of evaluating product proposals, a preliminary screening eliminates those of little or no apparent value to the company. Those remaining should be classified as speculative. As such, they are subject to more intensive analysis of their value to the company.

Potentially Profitable Phase

Ideas that are appraised as potential profit producers should be placed with other proposals waiting their turn on the development schedule. Positioning these in a special category calls attention to the fact that they have not been assigned a place in the development group's schedule. This is important. Good ideas, ones on which time and money have been spent in assessing their potential as profit producers, have failed to get into development schedules as a result of neglect and oversight. Positioning these in a special category reduces this risk.

Scheduled Phase

In the analysis of a product portfolio, projects awaiting development are a sign of management vigor in promoting new product programs. When too many projects are awaiting development, this fact may point up organizational weaknesses, such as inadequate development appropriations or staffing.

Developmental Phase

This is the phase in which ideas are turned into commercially feasible products. Everything that must be done to produce a salable product takes place here. Known facts are applied in developing the new product. Research is undertaken to supply new understanding to enhance product development. These facts and this understanding should encompass the physical sciences as well as economics and a fundamental knowledge of customer motivation.

Ideas and information are the raw materials in the development process. Salable merchandise is the end product of effectively applied technical talent. In between these two, the success of the business is largely determined. Second- or third-rate talent here will be reflected in competitive weaknesses of the final product. Products leaving the developmental phase should be ready for sale in every respect and, until ready, should remain under development.

To point up the fundamentals of analyzing a product line, the accompanying case study, "Troubleshooting A Product Program," reconstructs a typical situation. The problem faced at the close of the fiscal year by a hypothetical company will serve to illustrate the way in which a product portfolio can be put into significant perspective.

Troubleshooting a Product Program

At the close of the fiscal year, sales of the XYZ Company had increased steadily to a peak figure of $80,241,000. Contrasted with increased sales, however, after-tax profits were less than 6 percent—the poorest profit position company management had ever faced. To isolate factors contributing to declining profits, the performance of individual product lines themselves will be examined. Comparing individual product lines on the basis of their capacity to produce profits provides insight in interpreting profit trends.

Income Analysis

The overall product program of the company is built around ten basic product lines. Sales, profits, and other significant data for each product line are summarized in Table 4. Analysis of profits through these individual product lines is a basic management control, each product line being revealed as a profit producer or profit reducer. This analysis tells where to concentrate effort in improving the overall profit position.

Overall profits of the company for the year are 5.4 percent of sales. Product line D is the most profitable; six product lines show losses; three contribute negligible returns.

Each product line makes use of company resources, which should be deployed in the most productive manner. Here, more than half of the funds are seen to be unprofitably invested. Over 45 percent of the company's money is invested in product lines producing an unattractive return. In sharp contrast, the funds invested in a single product line produced the unusually favorable return of 45.3 percent on that investment.

Product Portfolio Analysis

Finding the problem areas will require a more probing analysis of each basic product line. To illustrate this approach, product line A will be examined in detail here. Product life phases will be considered in the same order already used.

Product line A consists of a group of the company's mechanical goods, centering on a line of reel-type mowers and including certain other auxiliary products that round out the product portfolio. Product-life-cycle relationships in this product line are shown in Exhibit 2.

Competitive. Four models of reel-type mowers are currently regarded as being in the competitive phase. These are models 72, 36, 85, and 29. They are positioned in the chart with respect to their own individual life cycle. Collectively, these four products account for a net income of $60,000. The net income attributable to each individual product is shown by the solid black bars in the lower section of the chart, just below the individual model. Figures at the top of each bar show the specific amount in thousands of dollars. For example, an $18,000 net income is allocable to the model 72 mower.

Obsolescent. Two products are classified in the obsolescent phase: Models 10 and 15 reel-type mowers. Together, they represent an income of $15,000.

Dropout. Products classified in the dropout phase account for $9,000 of the net profit from sales.

Introductory. New product offerings by the company cut across the range of competitive opportunities.

Table 4. Income analysis by product lines (thousand dollars).

Product Line	Sales			Manufacturing Cost		Sales and Administrative Costs		Profit or Loss			Capital Investment		
	% of Available Business	Dollars	% of Total Sales	Dollars	% of Total Manufacturing Effort	Dollars	% of Total S&A Effort	Dollars	% of Sales	% Return on Capital Investment	Dollars	% of Total Investment	Turnover of Total Investment
A	8	3,600	4.5	3,052	4.6	497	5.1	51	1.4	3.2	1,593	4.1	2.3
B	7	9,845	12.3	9,694	14.6	1,592	16.4	(1441)	-14.6	-49.6	2,903	7.5	3.4
C	12	9,700	12.1	8,228	12.4	1,700	17.5	(228)	-2.4	-3.8	5,990	15.6	1.6
D	21	36,900	46.0	26,356	39.8	3,388	34.8	7,156	19.4	45.3	15,800	41.0	2.3
E	16	4,845	6.0	4,030	6.1	909	9.3	(94)	-1.9	-11.5	819	2.1	5.9
F	14	2,200	2.7	1,851	2.8	347	3.6	2	.1	.1	1,795	4.7	1.2
G	18	1,975	2.5	1,829	2.8	141	1.4	5	.3	.4	1,259	3.3	1.6
H	15	5,925	7.4	5,587	8.4	513	5.3	(175)	-3.0	-4.3	4,033	10.5	1.5
I	11	2,950	3.7	3,327	5.0	368	3.8	(745)	-25.3	-26.9	2,774	7.2	1.1
J	8	2,301	2.8*	2,226	3.5*	280	2.8*	(205)	-8.9	-13.3	1,540	4.0	1.5
Total		80,241	100.0	66,180	100.0	9,735	100.0	4,326	5.4	11.2	38,506	100.0	2.1

* Adjusted to total 100 percent

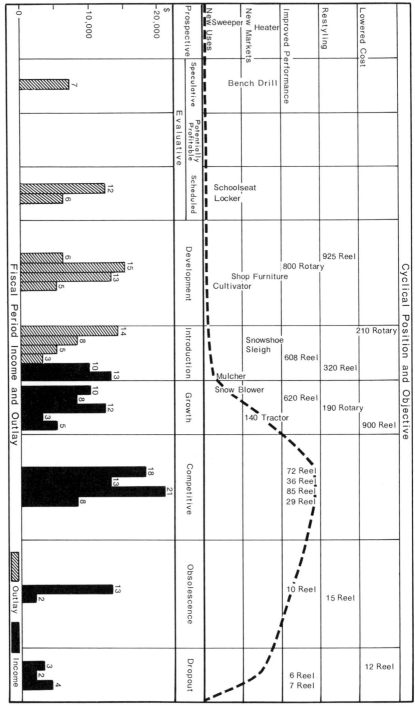

Exhibit 2. Product program analysis.

Lower cost. Model 210 rotary mower is a redesign of the Model 190 rotary and provides a comparable product at a lower cost, reflected in the selling price of the new items.

Restyling. Model 320 reel-type mower, which is being introduced to the market, represents a restyling of the Model 6 reel unit, which is scheduled for dropout.

Improved performance. The Model 608 reel-type mower represents a reengineering of the Model 15 reel unit, which is classified in the obsolescent phase. A dropout date has not yet been scheduled for the Model 15.

New markets. An attempt is being made to enter new markets having different seasonal characteristics. Snowshoes and sleighs are being added to the line to provide items in the product portfolio that will have off-season characteristics. Both snowshoes and sleighs have seasonal patterns running directly counter to the products in the present line, all of which are used during the summer.

New uses. Prior work with lawn mowers gave the company's engineers the experience needed to extend the usefulness of the product to leaf mulching.

Products in the introductory phase represent an outlay in excess of income of $7,000. Two of the products yield a profit of $23,000 but this is offset by the $30,000 outlay for the four remaining products in the introductory phase. It should be expected that products in this category will not show a profit. This is a market development phases.

Growth. Five products have entered the growth phase: a snowblower, a tractor, two reel-type mowers, and one rotary mower. In the current period shown in the chart, each of the five major competitive opportunities discussed previously is being exploited by products in the growth phase. This reflects the fact that considerably greater attention is being paid to product development in current periods than was the practice in earlier years. From a study of the classification of older products in the competitive, obsolescent, and dropout periods it is apparent that no attention was given to products for new markets or new uses. Primary emphasis was in the single direction of performance improvements in existing models with one attempt at restyling and one at design for lower cost.

Products in the growth phase currently yield an annual return of $38,000. Growth in sales is anticipated for each of these five items. The net return is expected to exceed $100,000 within a short period of a few years. New product development is not only making substantial contributions to the profits of the company but is broadening the profit base and contributing to stability.

Turning now from the in-market categories to the pre-market items, we can gain a further insight into the long-range strengths and weaknesses of the company's product program.

Prospective. In this program, there is a relative dearth of new ideas awaiting appraisal. Both a driveway and sidewalk sweeper have been proposed, as well as a workshop heater, but ideas for lower costs, restyling, and improved performance are noticeably lacking.

Speculative. The company has already spent $7,000 in evaluating a bench drill that would enable it to enter new markets. As yet, available evidence is inconclusive as a basis for either accepting or rejecting the proposal.

Potentially profitable. Analysis of this product portfolio shows that there are no unscheduled proposals. Those ideas that have appeared to be potential profit producers have been scheduled. Other than to accommodate the normal time required to process an idea into the development schedule, there isn't any good excuse for a backlog of unscheduled projects. Even though it may not be feasible to commence work on a project for several years, it should be scheduled. This in itself will call management's attention to the need for action to relieve the backlog of scheduled projects.

Scheduled. Two projects are in the scheduled phase, a school seat and a locker. An expenditure of $18,000 has been allocated to these two proposals. This money was actually disbursed in evaluating the merit of these respective proposals. Since the proposals themselves have moved into the scheduled phase, expenditure figures move with them.

Developmental. Four products are under development—a cultivator, shop furniture, a rotary mower, and a reel mower. An outlay of $39,000 has covered this development work during the period under review. It should be noted that no attention is being given to new products that will take advantage of cost-reduction opportunities in the present program. This neglect could have far-reaching consequences in the event that competitors plan to capitalize on such opportunities.

Planning for Tomorrow

Positioning individual products properly with respect to their own place in the life cycle will do more to reveal to engineers new needs than any other step that can be taken in evaluating the soundness of product programs.

In this age of steadily advancing technologies, top management is becoming increasingly aware of the rapidly growing need for dynamic product portfolio management. Product portfolio analysis is the starting point in planning for profits. The insight revealed by such analysis joined to that gained by perusing financial statements provides the perspective that turns words and numbers into meaningful facts and figures. It can be a potent tool both in evaluating present realities and projecting future ones.

11

Why
New Products Fail

A SHORT while ago a product manager proudly proclaimed he had never experienced failure with a new product program he had undertaken. This seemingly remarkable performance record probably proved tragically costly to his company. Those who have been successful with new product programs, those who have the greatest number of "hits" to their credit, have always experienced their fair share of product failures. The only way a product manager can score 100 percent is to play it so safe that he inevitably misses a lot of good bets.

Those who want to capture the profit potential inherent in new ventures must recognize in advance that they are going to make mistakes. In any kind of business the greatest gains are always inseparably linked to risk. Those who reorganize their new product group every time a venture fails to make the grade can't keep up with their more sophisticated competitors. Those who run successful new product programs regard a certain amount of failure as a built-in cost.

A mature approach to new product development is based on a clear recognition of the kinds of problems that have spelled failure for programs in the past. Knowing the pitfalls that may prove troublesome helps keep new product programs going in a direction that offers the best chance of bypassing these common hazards.

Not all new product failures are spectacular—the newly launched product may not sink immediately under the salvos of commercial warfare. Instead, it may just develop slow profit leaks that sink it before anyone is even aware there's trouble.

The experiences of a number of companies show that there are 12 primary reasons why new products fail. Perhaps a thirteenth could be added—fear of failure. A new product program can develop slow leaks and finally founder merely because everyone's afraid to act—and take the chance of making a mistake. After all, no one points a finger at those who stall for time.

Yet these uncertainties can be avoided and risks of product planning minimized at the same time. A lot can be learned by studying product failures, particularly these 12 main problems.

Timing Was Off

The best-planned programs can trip on timing. In new product planning, few things seem more certain than that there is a time and place for everything. Put another way, every part of a new product program must fit a master schedule.

To illustrate the importance of timing, here is how one company missed a market. The proposed new product was given the green light after careful appraisal and screening. It looked like a real money maker. It was a specialty item for the Christmas market, one accounting for 80 percent of the sales of this type of item. Two years was estimated as the time needed to develop the idea, get it into production, and fill the pipelines between producer and consumer. But unforeseen difficulties arose and delays resulted. Because the importance of tying the product's introduction to the Christmas market was overlooked, the delays weren't offset by extra effort. As a result, the market was missed by six weeks—six weeks that cost a loss of 80 percent of one year's sales.

In another case involving an industrial product, timing played a different role with equally costly consequences. One large manufacturer of electronic components planned to introduce a new tape-recording device adapted to visual images. Engineering development was allowed to lag and as a result, a competitor was the first to introduce the apparatus. It was quickly established as a recognized standard in the television industry.

Some delays can't be circumvented. No amount of attention paid to schedules can prevent the unforeseen from happening. But this isn't the function of schedules—their job is to highlight dates that have an important bearing on the profit picture. Then, when delays do occur, it will be possible to make a rapid appraisal of the probable cost of these delays and to relate this cost to the cost of offsetting them with accelerated programs.

Too much or too little, timed too soon or too late, can cause serious consequences. "Too little and too late" are among the saddest words heard in discussions of new product programs. Equally unfortunate is the opposite extreme of "too much and too soon." This can be just as costly! Timing is the important factor in avoiding these bugaboos of product planning.

Timetables are vital to the success of new product development. They should reflect a recognition that dates are coupled to dollar signs and that time periods are tied to costs. Compromises must be made, but once this is done the importance of these decisions should not be forgotten. Too often, careful planning efforts, once completed, are treated as an encumbrance left over from the past rather than as a guide to the future. When this happens, all of the effort that has gone into planning is wasted.

Departures from timetables should be viewed with alarm. They should signal the need for prompt program reappraisal. Timing is too closely tied to profits to be neglected.

The Product Wasn't Practical

Some good ideas just don't pass the test of commercial feasibility. It isn't always easy to distinguish between what can be done and what is commercially feasible. The difference between these two is the difference between profits and losses. It isn't enough to be able to produce the product; it must be possible to sell it at a profit.

Overlooking this fundamental consideration would seem to be almost impossible, but the challenge of technical achievement sometimes has a temporarily blinding effect. Individuals who are otherwise quite objective in their outlook frequently fail to be such when faced with the opportunity to score a technical triumph. From a business point of view, profits are the only ultimate triumph.

Failure to pass the test of commercial feasibility has come about in many ways. Here is a rapid rundown of some of the more familiar tales of woe:

It was easy to produce one, but we ran into difficulty with production lots.

It was a good product but it took us too long to tool up.

We didn't realize how much it would cost to develop the market.

We didn't understand what our customers really wanted.

The ultimate test of commercial feasibility lies in the answer to two questions: (1) Can it be made? (2) Can it be sold at a profit? Affirmative answers are needed.

Industrial products and consumer items incorporating advanced engineering technology are particularly sensitive to the test of commercial feasibility. The challenge of technical achievement has already been cited as one of the reasons why new products are pushed to completion without weighing all the factors. Beyond this is the difficulty of appraising the final product, with its highly complex technology, until that product actually takes shape. Performance characteristics are often critical in determining commercial feasibility. In many cases these can only be determined by building prototypes.

Customer Needs Changed

New products are created and developed in a dynamic environment. Carefully conducted surveys may reveal specific customer needs, but these needs can change before sufficient time has elapsed to capitalize on them.

The time involved in making a profit on a new product can be substantial. Products must not only be created, produced, and marketed, they must also enjoy a sufficient selling span to build an attractive return on the investment. If the risk is great that the span may be too short, it's a good idea to reappraise the situation.

Some years ago, a company concluded that there was a market for an electric razor-blade-sharpener. This was based on a carefully conducted study. By the time the product was developed, needs had changed. The price of razor blades had been drasticaly reduced. Ejector-type dispensers, which eliminated the handling of sharp blades, had become available. The introduction of the electric shaver had captured part of the potential market. The need to resharpen razor blades was largely eliminated.

One of the common errors in analyzing customer needs is to consider the survey completed once product development gets under way. During the development stage, more than ever before, it is important to maintain vigilance over potential markets. The investment in a new product mounts steadily during the development phase. When factors arise that alter sales prospects, they should be faced as soon as they appear. Nothing is gained by adopting ostrich-like tactics. Burying one's head in the sand provides no protection.

Action that has been taken and money that has been spent can't always be salvaged. But the early detection of new factors that change original assumptions prevents needless additional expenditures of time and energy. Programs can be altered to provide new direction. Resources can be diverted into more profitable channels.

Consumer needs are always changing. A steadily increasing watchfulness over these changes is needed as the investment in new products grows.

Basic Assumptions Were Forgotten

Every new product is based on specific assumptions. Here are some assumptions of one manufacturer in developing an automatic multipurpose machine tool:

1. An expanding market for automatic equipment
2. An opportunity to increase profits by entering this market
3. A desire to expand in this direction
4. A willingness to accept the added burdens on management's time

The engineering department embarked on the project. They came up with a special-purpose machine tool that integrated a time-consuming sequence of operations into one operation. The machine was marketed, none too promisingly. For some time, management's energies were dedicated to making a success of the project. Everyone is familiar with the flurry of activities when a company attempts to achieve such goals. Sales and engineering conferences, dealer meetings, and executive huddles occupy management's time to the hilt.

As frequently happens when the going gets rough, someone began to wonder how the company got into the muddle it was in. Some of the basic assumptions were recalled. In this case—an automatic multipurpose tool, to enhance future profits in an expanding market. The tool as developed didn't fit. Basic assumptions had been forgotten. It is easy to forget the assumptions on which decisions are made.

Engineers and scientists get lost in the details of their work and fail to check their directions periodically. They follow clues as they must, but fail to defer interesting leads that run counter to their more immediate objectives. Salesmen and marketing men are prone to lose interest in longer range developments once the enthusiasm kindled by a new idea has spent itself. Management is distracted by day-to-day activities.

New products are frequently neglected until it's too late. And they often stray far from their original direction because basic assumptions were forgotten.

Basic assumptions shouldn't be so rigid that they aren't adjustable to new intelligence as it develops. As new knowledge and information suggest changes in basic assumptions, the entire program—including the basic assumptions—should be reviewed. Changes should reflect new conditions and new needs, and basic assumptions should be altered only by informed action. Changes should never be a byproduct of neglect.

Goals Weren't Clearly Defined

The driving force behind successful new products lies in well-developed corporation objectives. Yet it's rare when executives are able to clearly state their companies' objectives. It's rarer still when these statements reach a common focus. Yet concentrated, coordinated effort depends on common goals. Lacking these, executives are apt to drive toward conflicting ends.

For example, the development group in one company spent sizable sums turning out a diversified product line while the sales group was concentrating on establishing a leadership position in a single industry market. In another case, a chemical company developed a food-processing operation subsequently judged too foreign to established business for further exploitation. With odds as unfavorable as they are to the success of any new venture, new products should have the benefit of coordinated efforts within the company if they are to have any chance of success.

Product managers work most effectively when goals are clearly defined and the goals are linked to corporate objectives. Indeed, these product goals are one of the most important facets of corporate objectives. Nothing is more important to business success than a company's products. And a continuing flow of new products is necessary to inject added vitality into the company's product lines.

New products frequently fail because of conflicts of interest within the company's own operations. The reason: confusion over objectives. When top management fails to establish objectives, this function is usurped by those in widely scattered activities at lower echelons. Goals established at these levels will be motivated by many factors, some good and some selfish. At best, they never achieve the objectivity and cohesion needed for successful new product planning, production, and promotion.

Product Competed with Customers' Sales

Products aren't always sold to the ultimate consumer. Numerous middlemen may be involved between an initial sale and the final customer. A fiber producer sells to a yarn producer, who in turn sells to a knitting mill, whose customer may be a converter. The chain doesn't stop there. Converters sell to wholesalers, who sell to apparel houses, who sell to distributors. Apparel then passes to retailers and finally to the ultimate consumer. There have been many customers for the original fiber. The fiber itself was probably produced from a chemical intermediary that had already passed through a number of sales sequences.

Thinking about new products is sometimes projected to things the company buys and sells. This is dangerous territory, particularly so because thinking turned into action can have a serious impact on currently profitable products. Competing with customers or suppliers may prove costly.

A company's customers and suppliers operate in markets having their own distinctive characteristics. In the various parts of the same industry, specialized experience and know-how must be acquired. Technologies may also be different. It's a mistake to assume that it's easy to expand in any direction from an established spot. Reputation may help, but profits will largely depend on good, hard work.

Invading the territory of customers and suppliers is an act of commercial warfare. Retaliatory measures must be anticipated. If you begin competing with customers for their markets, some of these customers may shift to other suppliers. This means lost sales that must be offset by additional orders from new markets yet to be exploited by relatively new selling teams. And in retaliation, customers and suppliers can expand their individual spheres of operation too!

Before developing new products that compete with those of customers or suppliers, the consequences should be carefully weighed.

Potential gains should be based on an evaluation of retaliatory strategies either defensive or, more important, offensive.

Failure to Recognize Opportunity

A number of years ago the president of a company that produced mechanical devices expressed an interest in developing a line of consumer items. His chief engineer proposed a multipurpose yard tool. He proposed that the comapny develop a lawn mower, powered by a gasoline unit, that could be removed and used to do other jobs when it wasn't driving the lawn mower. He pointed to a great many jobs such a unit could power in any household and to the part-time nature of jobs like grass cutting and snow removal.

Construction of a model was approved. The chief engineer's group developed a multipurpose power unit adapted to a snow blower, a cultivator, a compressor, hedge clippers, and other devices as well as to a lawn mower. Each could be used interchangeably with the one power unit.

Then the negative thinkers got to work. The power pack was too heavy for women to handle. Separate single-purpose drives for each tool would represent design optimums for the specific application. All the attachments would stand by every time the power unit had to be repaired. Finally, the "nays" won out. The project was dropped. Some years later the product was introduced by a competitor. An opportunity was lost by the company that first had the idea because it let negative thinking win.

Negative thinkers in another company have been picking ideas to pieces for over 15 years. During this time they have rejected over a dozen good ideas—ideas that have since proved to be successful for their competitors. One of a new idea's greatest weaknesses is precisely its newness. It's always easy to spot weaknesses, but only a few are capable of recognizing opportunities.

Turning new products into profitable commercial ventures calls for vision. It's easy to think of reasons why new products aren't any good, and the world abounds with men who know what's wrong with almost everything. But for the most part it's costly to listen to negative thinkers. They have nothing constructive to contribute. The real producers are the men who sense opportunity. These are the men who create profits, those rare individuals whose minds are triggered by new ideas, ideas that seem to set off a chain reaction of other ideas that can be developed, applied, and put to use. Success stems from opportunities recognized.

Inaccurate Market Measurement

No examination of product failures could overlook this cause of so many disasters. Undue optimism may lead to new products that don't succeed because the markets for them aren't adequate. Undue pessimism may result in rejection of ideas because market potentials aren't recognized. In either case, markets aren't properly appraised.

Competence in dealing with marketing problems comes only through intensive training and years of practice. A man who has a flair for marketing work must acquire both training and experience before his advice is worth very much. Without this background, the risk is great that markets will be misinterpreted. Market measurement has two major facets: (1) identification of specific markets, and (2) determination of the potential each holds for particular products.

The simple statement that a market hasn't been measured has many subtle implications. For example, if one has developed a new mechanical foot massager that might be used by either men or women, it's obvious that the market hasn't been measured just by counting all the men and women. To make the item profitable, one needs to know the relationship between sales volume, price ranges for the product, and other market characteristics. Market measurements must be spelled out in terms of real products and real customers. Equivocation is out of place in a market research report. Findings must be clearly stated as a basis for decisions that must be made and action that must be taken.

Then, too, difficulties in measuring markets are frequently traceable to failure in clearly establishing product specifications and parameters. A market analyst can establish with considerable certainty existing buying patterns. He can establish the fact that x number of people bought y number of $15 wristwatches last year in metropolitan centers of over one million people. With less certainty he can project the market's probable behavior in the ensuing year, if all other things remain equal. All other things won't remain the same, so the market analyst next makes an assumption and introduces more uncertainties.

The results are still useful. It's the next step that introduces a big factor of error. When the market analyst is asked to apply this data to a poorly defined product concept, the results he comes up with can't be any better than the established product specifications and parameters. Market analysts must have a clear picture of the product and its performance characteristics to construct a well-defined market profile.

When a market analyst is called on to construct a product image complete with specifications from his market studies, he is being asked to carry out an assignment considerably broader than simple market measurement. He needs specialized talents going far beyond those possessed by many marketing people. Lacking these talents, he may not translate his findings into a crystal-clear product picture. The net result—product failure.

To avoid this pitfall in product development, be sure that those who are measuring markets are appraising the market for the product that has been developed, not some marketing man's blurred image or misconception of what's on the drawing board. Market measurement must match product specifications. On the one hand, the market for a specific product must be measured. On the other, the market measurement must state the product characteristics for which the measures are valid.

Ignorance of Competitive Conditions

Someone once said, "There are none so blind as those who won't see!" There's a lot of wisdom packed into this simple saying. It highlights one of the underlying causes of new product failure.

Times are always changing. Changes in both the technological climate and the economic climate should be anticipated. Alert businessmen see change as creating opportunities to exploit new markets. Others regard change as one of the hazards of doing business. In either case, however, ignorance of competitive conditions causes product failures. Usually there isn't any good reason why technological developments and other competitive changes should come as a surprise to those who should be informed. Admittedly it takes time and money to keep up to date. It also takes talent. Notwithstanding, the cost of keeping up to date is relatively low. These costs are inexpensive insurance against surprise attacks on product programs.

Many new-product-program failures stem from not making use of readily available information. It may bolster one's morale to think that troubles resulted from scientific breakthroughs that couldn't be anticipated or came as a consequence of sudden moves by competitors, but this is rarely the case. Most technical developments take from five to ten years to reach commercial use. Competitors are seldom able to turn on the proverbial dime. Surprises come from a failure to stay informed.

To find out what's going on, you can't depend only on trade literature or science journals. In the competitive business climate, where changes take place rapidly, you must accept personal responsibility for gathering important news in particularly critical areas on a first-hand basis. The most successful people have an ability to anticipate news of importance to them. This extrasensory perception is a valuable asset, one developed by practice.

Overselling Product Proposals

Those responsible for product development programs point to two important ingredients of success—sound judgment and a willingness to accept risk as a cost of growth. Product development is both an art and a science. The art is practiced in striking a balance between drive and enthusiasm on the one hand and sound judgment as it relates to technology and management on the other.

No one can be certain of the point at which drive and enthusiasm oversell an idea. One test is to examine the degree of personal feeling involved. Enthusiasm shouldn't be due to highly personal feelings about a project. The continuance or discontinuance of product development programs shouldn't be regarded as reflecting on the abilities of those assigned to particular projects. If conditions change or facts become known making it advisable to drop a project, those concerned with the development shouldn't try to override good sound judgment just because of personal identification with the program. This kind of overselling proves costly.

Of course, those to whom responsibility for the development of a new product is assigned must have drive and enthusiasm to overcome the many obstacles that may arise. But when this personal momentum gets out of bounds and is used to promote projects in the face of sound reasons for discontinuing them, overselling creeps into the picture. Products that are oversold usually fail sooner or later. It's better to take losses as early as possible.

Incompatibility with the Line

A company can successfully compete with its own line of products, but only on the basis of carefully thought-out product strategies. Competition can take many forms. One company, as the result of a planned strategy, competed with itself for years in the sale of electric clocks in identical price brackets. It did this to crowd out competition. Another company has an economy line of products similar to its established brand but sold under a different brand name. Large retail outlets often sell products under their own private labels, products that compete with standard brands in the same retail outlet. This kind of competition reflects careful planning.

Incompatibility arises in other ways, too. Successful product lines are the result of competent creative design, engineering, production, sales and service activity, and a management that understands the product line. Attempts to fit radically different product concepts into the company's product portfolio may call for such changes in thinking that these new products reduce the effectiveness of these different functions.

Similar products in two or more price brackets have also introduced problems when strategies weren't thought through in advance. Products intended to appeal to two markets may be compared by discerning buyers in higher price brackets. Buyers may decide that price differentials go beyond performance differentials. Volume sales may swing to economy products whose price is made possible only by the allocation of basic costs to higher priced products. Such shifts may subsequently result in price increases. Customer goodwill may be lost and products may fail because of incompatible product lines.

Disparity in Supply and Demand

A product can fail because customers can't buy it. Too long a period of time between the announcement of a new product and its availability to customers affects markets in different ways. Costly promotional campaigns lose their effectiveness. By the time the product is available, customers have forgotten all about it.

Situations where supply isn't integrated with demand play into competitors' hands in a different way. The longer it takes to get a new product into the hands of customers, the more time competitors have to assess markets and develop competitive offerings.

Not only must direct supply lines to customers be filled and integrated with demand, but new products must be available in advance to sales organizations. When a company has a great number of sales outlets, a substantial supply of a new product may be necessary simply to fill these pipelines.

Then, too, service facilities must precede new products if they are to be kept in working order. When a product is new, it's important to handle service complaints quickly to prevent customer dissatisfaction from growing.

All of these factors are tied together. They must be pursued simultaneously with the end objective of integrating supply and demand. How many times has a salesman been unable to answer all of your questions about a new product? How many times have products been advertised that couldn't be purchased because no one knew where to buy them? How many times has difficulty been encountered in obtaining repair parts or accessories for the new products? Each reflects a failure to integrate supply and demand. Each, if it happens enough times in enough places to enough people, results in new product failures.

These 12 problem areas have resulted in disaster for new products in the past—and they no doubt will in the future. By being aware of particularly troublesome causes of product failures, companies can plan strategies to avoid them. Most of those who have experienced difficulties in these particular problem areas have stumbled into them blindly. Forewarned is forearmed in dealing with them.

Avoiding the common hazards of developing new products calls, first, for recognition of the problem itself; second, for a willingness to plan strategies to avoid potential pitfalls; and third, for the determination to put planned programs into action. While a lot of work is involved, the results can prove rewarding. On the other hand, neglect may result in product failures that wipe out all the time, effort, and money invested in the new product.

12

Checkpoints in
New Product Pioneering

DRAMATIC successes await companies that have built carefully planned, active programs for new product pioneering. An analysis of nearly any product group will reveal the pioneer product—the innovation—and the copies subsequently produced by others.

Today, the pioneering of products represents an area of management endeavor in which the horizons are unlimited. In spite of this, many companies have not been successful with new product programs. This can usually be traced to a feeling by executives that they do not have enough appreciation of the problems involved to effectively administer new programs. This feeling is intensified in many companies by a lack of mutual understanding between top management and the technical people responsible for these programs.

Planning a program and getting it started are only half the job. Maintaining a running check throughout the development phases and steering the program to a successful conclusion are even more important. When a program flounders, those concerned—management, engineers, scientists, sales people—must know what remedial steps to take.

A management with experience from successful new product programs has learned to delineate the various steps in product development and has devised checks at each point to measure progress. The questions asked at these steps can provide other firms with insight into problem areas that often prove to be stumbling blocks. If these same questions are asked during steps in any new product development, most disasters can be circumvented. Managers must know how a typical program is broken down into steps, how the checkpoints are set up, and what action should be taken.

Development Phases

A new product, or the redesign of a going product, passes through five phases before it reaches the ultimate customer: evaluation, application, commercialization, production, distribution. While these phases are easily identified, boundaries between phases are difficult to distinguish. An overlap between activities and a continuous feedback of information are characteristic.

Control points are established to measure the evolution of a concept into the hardware of a commercial product. At each of these control points management should measure progress by asking the right questions. Those responsible for the program should know what questions to expect and should be prepared to supply authoritative answers.

Evaluation

1. *What do we know about it?* Answers to this question form the groundwork for all further investigation. The data that must be gathered and evaluated includes prior history, market estimates, and technical feasibility. All accumulated knowledge should be reviewed and brought up to date in the light of current technical, economic, and competitive developments. The latest information on patent situations and a current literature survey should be included. The importance of this step cannot be overstressed.

2. *Shall we try?* All the thinking that has developed must be applied to answer this question. At the outset it is relatively easy to maintain an analytical attitude. This becomes much more difficult as time goes on. Interesting facets develop that attract personal attention and that destroy impartiality. The information gathered to support this decision must be completely unbiased and open to question, and must remain so. The individuals involved must be prepared to support their decisions in discussions that may become both partial and heated.

3. *How long will it take?* Ideas develop into products through the use of available money, manpower, and machines. Since few com-

panies have any of these in surplus, schedules must be established to determine the time-cost relationship. While a short development time may run up costs due to inefficiencies, longer development periods may sacrifice marketing opportunities. Reasonable estimates of development time require schedules that balance timing with associated costs of resources necessary to implement the program. Accurate time estimates are essential and should be followed closely.

4. *Will it pay to do it?* This question must be answered by an educated guess based on investigation of practicability of the product, nature and size of the market, sales methods, manufacturing requirements, management and organizational requirements, and the profit potential. It is far less expensive in the long run to spend time and money to fully define every aspect of the situation than to uncover facts later that require backtracking. Because of the many intangibles involved, all possible facts must be marshaled for use. Decisions based on guesses can be costly.

Application

5. *What can we discover?* Before prototype construction, the mechanical aspects of the new product should be rechecked. After this final review, the product is then completely engineered with the expectation that it will become a production item. The latest technological developments should be studied and included where practicable to offset the possibility of rapid obsolescence. All practical ideas and suggestions should be gathered, studied, evaluated, and, when possible, used. Except for debugging and modification, this concludes the engineering development process.

6. *Will it work?* Without an operating model, very little of the new product is tangible. At the earliest time consistent with research and engineering programs, an operating breadboard model should be constructed in order to prove out any innovations or departures from previous practice. The general objective is to prove the practicability of the product. Tests should be designed that check out the intended functions and measure how satisfactorily these functions are performed.

7. *How shall we build it?* When the functional requirements of the model have been decided on, the actual engineering and construction can begin. The model should reflect a realistic relationship between available materials, operating principles, and established requirements. A very strong effort should be made to include as many of the final desirable features as possible, such as ease of maintenance and operation. The next phase is commercial evaluation.

Commercialization

8. *Shall we go ahead?* Once ideas approach the pilot stage, management takes a greater interest. Questions become more pointed and answers are expected to be more specific. Management recognizes that it must decide about pilot runs to gather additional manufacturing and marketing data. This, in turn, will again increase the investment. Seeing the model in physical form will stimulate exploration of its potential. While management is thinking out loud, much can be learned from its reactions that will be of value in planning and preparing for subsequent developments.

9. *Does it have everything?* The model built earlier was built to provide functional performance. In this phase, a final prototype is built, one that must perform for the customer under actual operating conditions and duplicate the product to be offered for sale in every way except method of manufacture. Naturally, first consideration must be given to performance since the produce must do the job for which it is intended. The customer must be pleased. After the purchase, servicing must be taken into consideration. Costs must be kept in line since the selling price will influence both sales volume and profits.

10. *How does it look?* Development of the prototype should be undertaken with a this-is-it attitude. All available data relating to problems that may be encountered in production, distribution, performance, and servicing should be digested and the final solutions incorporated in the prototype. Once it has been completed, management, production people, sales personnel, distributors, dealers, buyers, and others will review it and comment on it. Although unanimous approval is rare, this is the stage at which top management decisions must be made and final approval secured.

11. *Does it work?* Criteria for sound performance are based on knowledge of how the customer will use the device. Firsthand knowledge is required—not theory. Unless customer-service requirements are kept in mind, tests will be too severe in some cases and inadequate in others. The former results in overdesigning, the latter in performance failure. Either extreme will prove costly and may kill the anticipated profit potential. The performance tests to which the product is subjected must not only be thorough but must duplicate actual customer operating conditions.

12. *Can the customer make it work?* Prototypes should be tested by putting them in the hands of customers for actual use. The results of field tests are varied, interesting, and instructive, but above all they prove the adequacy—or inadequacy—of a new design. The engi-

neers who have lived with a product and are familiar with it are frequently completely unable to imagine the manner in which the customer will put it to work. Only field tests can establish the real performance limits of the product and the adequacy of the design. The results of these tests are then gathered and analyzed for use.

13. *How can it be improved?* Since prototypes rarely pass all performance tests, the test results must be evaluated to determine new design requirements. Successful products are generally evolutionary; thoroughness, persistence, and patience during the development phase are keys to a soundly designed, competitive product. Time and money spent in perfecting designs reap tremendous savings in what would otherwise be delays and charges for in-production changes. Eagerness to get the product on the market must not be permitted to overrule development of sound designs or incorporation of improvements.

14. *Will manufacturing modify it?* When a satisfactory prototype has evolved, it must be turned over to the production people, even if it is not easy to take it away from the engineers, who may well see more work to be done. Review and modification for low-cost production include changes suggested by available production equipment and know-how and by consideration of purchased parts, subassemblies, and materials. If these proposed changes leave prior performance test results open to question, the tests must be repeated. Experience gained before should simplify and speed up the new tests.

15. *How does it look now?* Final models represent thoroughly worked-over designs ready for approval by all concerned. Such comments as these must be expected: Sales manager, "Price too high, insufficient styling." Production manager, "Hard to build." Engineers, "Not ready yet—rushed too much." Accountant, "Costs too high." Purchasing, "Can buy complete for less money." Watchmen, "That thing still here?" These comments must be taken philosophically. Since good men can and want to do better, this is a healthy condition. At about this point, the model is finished and production planning begins.

Production

16. *How do we make it?* Manufacturing personnel keep costs of both time and money in mind when processing a new design. The lowest-per-piece cost may require entirely new production facilities with single-purpose machinery and tooling. Getting the product on the market in the shortest possible time may suggest simple tooling and the use of existing facilities only. The optimum solution is usually somewhere between these two extremes and requires the best in plan-

ning and projecting of eventualities. Plans must be left flexible to meet future requirements.

17. *Do we make or buy?* Products can be manufactured or purchased, in whole or in part, and both methods are normally used. Determination of the proper course requires a careful study of each individual part of the product. If the product was designed for the firm's own facilities, alternative designs of some parts may be considered for cost purposes. Purchasing as an alternative to manufacturing frequently raises concern over utilization of fixed investment. However, net cost per piece should be the determining factor. Buying may require minor design revisions.

18. *What are total costs?* The final cost of a new product is the sum of manufacturing costs and the cost of purchased components. This figure is used in developing the optimum selling price for the product and must be based on sound costing practices. If the costs are in line with the proposed sales price, all well and good. If not, stop here. Everything before is part of the process of developing a salable product. If the costs are not right, sales volume will be adversely affected and this in turn will raise the costs and squeeze profit margins. Too high costs may kill the project.

19. *How many for a trial run?* Pilot production provides limited quantities of a new product for market development without incurring the full investment of production tooling. Thus products can be proved out under actual sales and operating conditions at minimum cost. Sales experience must be gained to evaluate customer acceptance. If the response to the product is favorable, demand may develop with unexpected rapidity. Pilot runs permit maintaining small stocks until full production can get started. While plans and programs are being turned into facilities, the product passes into the distribution phase.

Distribution

20. *Do sales justify production?* The sales program for pilot-run products should be constructed in the same manner used for full-scale selling, and potential buyers should be unaware of the experimental nature of the program. This approach provides effective data for evaluating selling and marketing approaches. Because final production release calls for a major investment and changes are costly and difficult, the pilot run and initial market test must provide all data necessary for evaluating the soundness of the new product program and to establish production levels if the green light is given.

21. *How good is our sales and service?* A fundamental considera-

tion in setting up distribution channels is to achieve the most profitable way of making the product available in the quantities needed when and where the buyer is ready to purchase. The selling group must be ready to take over and sell the product as it rolls off the assembly line. The timing of sales and advertising is important to assure availability of merchandise as demand is created. Provision for servicing the product must be set up before it is offered for sale on a wide scale. Rapid and efficient customer service is needed.

22. *When do we start?* In one sense, manufacture begins with a turning of the wheels, but in an equally real sense the process began much earlier. The success of the "wheel-turning" phase is so dependent on preceding steps that it is itself of minor significance. The unfolding of programs planned in the previous stages of new product development reveals the time at which effective and economical production can begin. However, if earlier steps were slighted, costs will be incurred that may ruin eventual profitability and force abandonment of the product.

23. *How is it doing?* Problems encountered after new products are released for production and sale can seldom be solved by treating them as isolated cases. Somewhere, somehow, an essential step has been overlooked or poorly executed. The steps in the entire program may have to be retraced and all subsequent work reprogrammed. Every possible effort should be made to quickly solve problems as they arise and to locate their origin in the planning phases. Careful reassessment may head off subsequent difficulties, costly delays, and lost sales. Sound development programs bring success.

These 23 checkpoints help assure management that new product concepts are being transformed into salable products—that ideas are being turned into dollars.

13

Sharpening Up Decision Making

A PROPOSAL to spend some of the company's money on a program is placed on an executive's desk. The decision he makes may very well determine the whole course of an organization's overall effectiveness.

Now, what should he do? What kind of a decision should he make? How should he go about making it? These questions and other important ones arise whenever a proposal is placed on the desk of the man who has to make the final decision.

When some course of action is presented for approval, almost everyone starts right out by analyzing this proposal in order to find out what it's all about, how much it would cost, what it proposes to produce in return, and how long it would take. Experience warns us not to fall into the trap of making decisions before proposals have been put in their proper perspective.

Experience also points to the importance of taking four steps that sharpen up decision making. The results are rewarding.

First, develop a decision-making profile, the list of what's needed to reach objectives. Second, search out alternative courses of action that could be followed in reaching objectives. Third, define targets, timetables, and tactics. Fourth, establish a meeting of minds with respect to action to be taken.

Of itself, decision making isn't difficult; it's a matter of doing the obvious. The difficulty lies in defining the obvious. Directed effort is the basic ingredient in effective decision making. To define the obvious for decision-making purposes, decision makers must turn aimless activity into effort directed at developing a realistic pattern of needs by following through on the steps outlined above.

Develop a Decision-making Profile

In sharpening up decision making, the first question to ask is: "What's the frame of reference imposed by requirements?" When you go to a supermarket or department store without preparing a shopping list, you generally come back with an odd assortment of packages. True, you will have some of the things required, but you will have overlooked others. What's even worse, you may come back with things you don't even want, things bought on impulse. You can make another trip to pick up the things you overlooked, but time and money will have been wasted.

This familiar situation points up what happens when you make decisions before preparing a "shopping list." Decision-making profiles eliminate "impulse buying" in decision making. The development of profiles calls for a careful scrutiny of four factors.

First, specific needs must be met. Decisions must be considered in connection with needs. Certain things are essential in the interest of overall effectiveness.

Second, there are new things to be achieved. Goals go beyond immediate needs. Decisions made to meet needs merely put out "brush fires" and maintain going operations. Decisions made to meet goals determine what will be done in the days to come.

Third, the competitive climate creates a condition to be considered. Things ruled out earlier, for one reason or another, assume importance when competitors move in unanticipated directions. Decision makers must be sensitive to the competitive climate and correspondingly responsive.

Fourth, capabilities must be considered. One may profitably capitalize on opportunities to do things different from those being done, new things that make use of highly developed capabilities.

A sharply structured decision-making profile provides the frame of reference for decision making. It's a dynamic frame of reference, not a static one. Needs, goals, competition, and capabilities change with time and must be continually reviewed, reevaluated, and redefined to keep decision-making profiles current.

The four factors entering into the decision-making profile are interrelated. One factor can't be isolated from its relationship with the other three. For example, goals always reflect capabilities and day-to-day needs as well as the opportunities and pressures created by competition. In the same way, capabilities are byproducts of goals, needs, and the competitive climate. Inevitably, there will always be a high degree of homogeneity in the makeup of the factors entering into the decision-making profile.

Search Out Alternatives

The second question to ask is "What alternative courses of action are available?" Don't waste time weighing the pros and cons of taking a particular course of action until after searching out the available alternatives. Before trying to arrive at a "to do or not to do" decision, ask the questions, "What different courses of action could be taken to achieve some specific objective?" and "Which of these appears optimum?"

Try to turn any question of the kind that asks, "Should we do this or not?" into the kind of question that asks, "Should we do this or that?" or, better still, "Which of these alternatives should we select as a course of action?"

Applying this to the kind of personal decision you may be called on to make points up the pitfall that lies in making decisions before exploring available alternatives. For example, in discussing this year's vacation, you might ask the family, "How about going to Atlantic City?" Attention is immediately focused on Atlantic City, its attractions, the cost of going there, and the question of whether or not the family thought they might enjoy Atlantic City's attractions.

These are important considerations, certainly, but in another sense they're premature. A most important step has been omitted—the exploration of available vacation spots. The real starting point for any intelligent decision making in this case would be to ask, "Where might we spend our vacation?" Omit this step, and as you unpack your bags on returning from Atlantic City, you may wonder why you didn't go someplace you had just then thought of that would have made a better vacation spot than Atlantic City.

Analyzing available alternatives is important in all kinds of decision making. At the outset, try to turn every decision away from a process of saying yes or no to a specific proposal into a process of selecting the best course of action from among a number of proposed courses of action. Nothing is lost. You can still reject all the proposals if none seems suitable.

Define Targets, Timetables, and Tactics

The third question to ask is "What targets, timetables, and tactics are imposed?" These provide guidelines for decisions and action. To sharpen up decision-making targets, you must adequately define timetables and tactics.

Target definition for decision making purposes should encompass

1. Overall objectives
2. Resource allocations
3. Phase objectives
4. Review and reappraisal points
5. Cost commitments
6. Byproduct benefits
7. Probability of success

Careful consideration of each of these seven facets of targeting sharpens up decision making.

1. Statement of overall objectives. This answers the question "What is the decision expected to accomplish?" To be on the safe side, don't just ask the question, test the answer. Raise this question: "If this objective is achieved, will those involved be 100 percent satisfied?" If the answer to the second question isn't an unqualified yes, why not do something that will deliver what's wanted?

A statement of objectives should highlight those things that, if achieved, will satisfy all concerned. Every important qualification having any bearing on the end product of decisions should be included in the statement of objectives. It defines what's wanted. It tells those who are going to use the end products of decisions exactly what they are going to get. It tells others what's being done.

2. Relation to resources allocated. Every decision to do something places demands on available resources. A decision's relationship to available resources should be clearly defined. Answers to the questions "What is the return on the investment involved?" and "How soon?" are always important.

3. Objectives by phases. Those responsible for results want to take a look at what's going on from time to time. There are certain points in every program when performance can be evaluated. At other times it's almost impossible for anyone except those working daily with the details to tell what's going on.

Proposed programs should be broken down into action areas or phases. Terminal phase points come at those times when results can be clearly defined and measured—quantitatively as well as qualitatively. Results to be produced at terminal phase points should be summarized. Criteria reflecting a job well done at each terminal phase point should be clearly stated.

4. *Review and reappraisal points.* As terminal phase points are reached, initial decisions should be reviewed and reappraised. Decisions involve assumptions. All the facts needed to prejudge proposed programs before action takes place are rarely available. But as action does take place, data is developed that puts decisions in a different perspective. Unanticipated problems as well as opportunities are revealed. Review and reappraisal points provide a place to realign programs and thinking with reality as new information is developed.

Review and reappraisal points also provide opportunities to keep decisions focused on objectives and objectives aligned with practical potentials, as well as giving those responsible for decision making a chance to speak up before further action takes place. Review and reappraisal points provide managers with a further opportunity to manage. Hindsight ceases to be the hallmark of management acumen when those responsible for action areas exercise managerial foresight.

5. *Cost commitments.* Every decision has a built-in cost of some kind. Costs should be established for each action area and agreed on at the outset. It isn't enough to reach agreement on an overall cost figure. Expenses are always subject to scrutiny. Cost objectives should be established for each significant action area. Reviews of costs should be tied to terminal phase points rather than made monthly, quarterly, or semiannually. These times are usually not the times when action has reached the point where performance can be best measured for management decision making.

6. *Byproduct benefits.* Byproduct contributions to other programs should be outlined in terms of where these are expected to originate, on what basis, when, and what contribution is anticipated. The failure to clarify thinking about these potential benefits, preliminary to making decisions, is a serious error of omission.

7. *Probability of success.* A program's probability of success should be established in advance of decision making. If one or more of the critical action areas has a highly questionable chance of success, the outcome of the entire program will have this risk, too.

Careful consideration of each of these seven facets of targeting sharpens up decision making. Along with targets, timetables require definitive treatment. Targets are always accompanied by timetables. There are immediate matters and matters having long-range implications. Within this spectrum the range between too soon and too late may vary widely. It may be measured in minutes, days, or years, but a range exists for each decision.

Contemplated action must be reviewed in conjunction with an appropriate timetable. Effective action is action at the optimum point between the extremes of too soon and too late.

Targets and timetables are also linked with tactics. The tactics employed must be consistent with other activities. Decisions to do something can't disregard the impact, favorable or unfavorable, of the way in which other activities are carried out. For the most part the successful outcome of any action is dependent on its fitting in with the going way of doing things. Decision makers must determine what tactics are imposed on each action area.

The time taken to establish targets, timetables, and tactics should give decision makers guidelines that sharpen up decisions. It's part of the process of turning aimless activity into directed effort.

Develop a Meeting of Minds

The fourth question to ask in sharpening up decision making is "What is the consensus of those concerned as to the decision to be made?" The consensus of those sponsoring proposals, those responsible for action areas, and those who will apply the end products of a decision should be brought into focus. This gives all concerned an opportunity to reflect specific interests for which each is individually responsible. Equally important is the desirability of maintaining a balance between specific interests.

Time taken to arrive at a meeting of minds is time saved many times over. False starts are eliminated. Second guessing is avoided. The Monday morning quarterback, the man who can always explain what should have been done, is given his opportunity to call the play before it is made. The elimination of this troublesome problem alone is sufficient reason for reaching advance agreement before initiating any action.

There are a number of reasons why everyone concerned with decisions to be made, those sponsoring proposals, those responsible for action areas, and those responsible for applying the end product of decisions should take time for a meeting of minds with respect to targets, timetables, and tactics before decisions are made.

1. *To provide desired end results.* It's a good idea to make sure that everybody is seeking the same end results. Those responsible

for action should have the assurance that if they deliver specific results they will have satisfied the needs of those concerned. If those concerned can't agree on specific end results before programs are undertaken and can't define these end results in terms clear to all concerned, decisions should be held in abeyance until this can be done.

2. *To schedule review and reappraisal points.* Decision makers need to know how far to go before reviewing the data developed and realigning programs in accordance with findings. On Monday morning most men can call the plays that would have spelled victory for Saturday's game; today's Confederate generals have won the war many times over. Hindsight is always more powerful than foresight. Decision makers can offset the problems created by this kind of thinking by insisting on a meeting of minds with regard to review and reappraisal points.

3. *To validate objectives and point up necessary modifications.* Having spelled out the kind of results to be expected and having decided how far it is safe to go before taking another look, the decision makers should again review and confirm overall objectives. Now is the time to make sure that specific details are consistent with objectives. The purpose of a meeting of minds isn't to introduce rigidity, but flexibility. It's to tailor decisions to needs. This is the time to make changes. At this point change can be introduced without a loss of time or money. Later changes will be costly in terms of both. Specific questions that should be asked and answered at this point are these: What are the reasons for the decision? What output is expected? Is this consistent with the reasons for initiating the decision?

4. *To establish feasibility of proposals.* If a high element of risk is involved, it should be recognized. Decisions involve varying degrees of risk. Risk may involve a lack of adequate technical data, economic uncertainties, and legal considerations, to name just a few possibilities. The reason for reaching advance agreement with regard to the feasibility of proposed action is to acquaint everyone having any responsibility for carrying out decisions with all the factors involved so that each can contribute his best thinking.

5. *To assure quality consistent with requirements.* Men can do what's wanted, but when they don't know exactly what's wanted, refinements in the way they work may not match requirements.

6. *To define specific areas of interest and rank them in order of priority.* This will guarantee that what should come first will come first.

7. *To monitor time and cost factors and hold both to a minimum.* Sponsors and those responsible for carrying out decisions should agree

in advance both on overall timing and costs and timing and costs associated with each of the action areas. These can't be monitored effectively unless agreement is reached before decisions are made.

8. *To achieve maximum coordination and cooperation.* Individuals work at cross-purposes unless they are in complete agreement about what's to be done and what criteria are a measure of effective action.

9. *To plan alternate courses of action.* Advance agreement should be reached to avoid delays when programs encounter roadblocks. Time that would be otherwise wasted is saved by reaching advance agreement with regard to alternative courses of action that should be followed under specific circumstances.

Good decisions are managed, not made. They are based on the involvement of those concerned with the outcome of decisions, those concerned with carrying out the steps needed to turn decisions into action, those affected by the decisions themselves, and those initiating proposals.

For the most part, failure is the result of not doing what was wanted because someone didn't know what was wanted. Good decisions reflect the thinking of those involved and define what's wanted and what's considered feasible by those involved in the outcome.

part three
Organizing

14

Detecting and Defining Potentially Profitable Technology

IT can be said without equivocation that any corporation can achieve its goals, on time, and within cost limits established in advance. The management know-how is available to everyone. Yet only a few will make use of what's available to all. These few are those who make decisions that turn thoughts into action.

Learning the Lessons Taught by Experience

Management guidelines are established by practices with a good track record. The practices that have proved profitable for those who have been successful provide good guidelines for others to follow. At the same time the experience of those who seem to have proved that they didn't know how to do a good job affords a basis for cross-checking what's been learned from successful experience. There isn't any other sound basis for management guidelines.

Some time ago the man responsible for new products in a company that has one of the best records of success in capitalizing on new technology called attention to what he considered to be the secret of his company's success. He said: "Oh, it's quite simple, we just ask the right questions. Most people make mistakes because they haven't asked the right questions."

Here are some of the right questions that successful managers of technical programs ask in detecting and defining potentially profitable technology.

What Are the Discontinuities?

We might rephrase this question in these words: What do we know we can't do? Or we might ask: Where has thinking stopped? Answers to these two questions highlight discontinuities.

Two kinds of discontinuities are of interest to us: technological discontinuities and utilization discontinuities. Both are worth exploration in breadth and depth.

First, look at the consequences of some technological discontinuities. If the thinking of scientists and engineers in the thirties was correct, Texas Instruments doesn't exist today because the crystal detector had no future after the development of the vacuum tube. In the early days of radio when the crystal set gave way to the vacuum tube, scientists and engineers were in general agreement that they had seen all there was to be seen in the direction in which they were looking with regard to the crystal detector. They shifted all their attention to the vacuum tube and then gas-filled tubes. Today it's obvious that they missed by a mile in their thinking through their failure to recognize and concentrate on discontinuities in technology.

Take another example. For as far as we can look back, the attempt to develop a better pocket timepiece has been reflected in thinking largely focused on the balance wheel, the hairspring, and the mainspring. For years no one gave much thought to the probability of technological discontinuities. Even the first step taken in the development of a product as revolutionary as the electric wristwatch merely represented the replacement of the mainspring with a battery; it was not accompanied by any other significant changes in the system.

Finally scientists and engineers at the Bulova Watch Company explored the possibility of replacing the mainspring, gear train, and balance wheel with a tuning fork because the tuning fork is a far more accurate timing standard. At the time, the experts in tuning fork science, the scientists in Bulova's own American Time Products Division, told them it was an exercise in futility because there was no way to tap the tuning fork's power for productive purposes. A very profitable product, the Accutron watch, driven by a tuning fork, proved the experts to be victims of their own inability to bridge discontinuities in technology. They were victims of knowing what couldn't be done.

Still another example is given us by the scientists and engineers who dismissed all thought of practical applications of the phenomenon of thermoelectricity because there was no way to tap the power of the thermocouple. A so-called law of physics, the Wiedemann-Franz relationship, told them it was a job that couldn't be done. Good conductors of electricity were good conductors of heat. Subsequently, scientists questioned the validity of the Wiedemann-Franz relationship and came up with a new generation of thermoelectric generators that are very effective power producers. It's interesting to observe the fact that the scientists and engineers who harnessed thermoelectricity weren't the ones who had spent their careers working within the conventional confines of expert thinking about thermoelectricity. They weren't too familiar with what couldn't be done.

One more example will help to fix our focus on scientific discontinuities and their significance. The gyroscope has been the basic reference plane for inertial platforms and their predecessors since the time such a device has had any significance. Programs having as their purpose the improvement of inertial systems have concentrated on some very sophisticated approaches to frictionless, miniaturized masses moving at remarkably high speeds. At the same time, relatively little thinking was diverted to the exploration of opportunities that might be created by technological discontinuities. All the attention was focused on the apparent fact that the reference plane had to be a spinning mass; it couldn't be done any other way. Yet those who didn't know this subsequently capitalized on the Doppler effect between two light beams as a sensing system to indicate a change in motion.

Bridging each of these discontinuities resulted in products that performed old functions in a better way and products that produced new profits for the company. Similar opportunities are found in the form of utilization discontinuities.

If Eastman Kodak's fundamental premise—that people always want a negative so they can have extra prints made—had been correct, there would have been no market for a Polaroid camera. But people don't seem to know they always want a negative and so they go on buying Polaroid cameras. Dr. Land was successful with his Polaroid camera because he didn't know that the experts knew that he couldn't sell a camera that didn't produce a negative.

After every company in the typewriter industry passed up the patents for an electric typewriter, IBM, which wasn't even in the typewriter business, bought the patent from the inventor and produced an electric typewriter that captured the most profitable segment of the typewriter market because IBM didn't know that you couldn't sell an electric typewriter. IBM followed this up quickly by introducing the second major innovation in the industry in half a century, the interchangeable "Selectric" font. Recognizing a need for a typewriter with different type faces available to the secretary, IBM applied a system used in the Simplex typewriter more than a quarter of a century earlier to meet modern-day needs. Not having been in the typewriter industry for half a century, IBM didn't know what couldn't be done.

For many years scientists and engineers in the office copier industry regarded the photographic process as the ultimate answer to making one or two copies of a document. Everyone used the familiar photostat machine. From the photostat the thinking about the office copier jumped the utilization discontinuity to the mimeograph, the spirit duplicator and the gelatin process that turned out 25 or so copies. All such duplicators depended on transferring ink from one sheet of paper to another. All were geared to a need for multiple copies from a specially prepared master copy. But the industry overlooked the need for a process that would produce from one to ten copies of an original document in a dry, immediately usable form. This potential market was not being met by any available method. It represented a utilization discontinuity.

Chester Carlson, the inventor of the Xerox process, recognized this need. Not having been in the business of making office copiers, he didn't think along the same lines as the office duplicator expert. His thinking wasn't tied to conventional printing-ink technology. He thought in terms of triboelectricity, photoluminescence, and electron conduction. These concepts were foreign to the thinking of those familiar with office-copier-industry technology.

No established company that was producing office copying equipment would buy his invention. They didn't recognize the profit opportunity because he had bridged a utilization discontinuity. The experts knew that there was no market for what we recognize today as the very successful Xerox process. Chester Carlson and those who organized the Xerox Corporation lacked the wealth of experience that would have told them it couldn't be done.

The success of Xerox, IBM, and the Polaroid camera highlights an interesting aspect of discontinuities. It's this: The fresh approach in capitalizing on opportunities in every industry may be made by someone outside the industry. When a company's management is sure it knows all the answers to all the questions about the technologies related to its interests, the markets for its products, and the nature of its competition, it's in trouble.

Once someone is sure he has all the answers he stops giving any further thought to updating his thinking. A company and its industry are therefore both in trouble—because times change. Here are just a few of the products developed outside of companies and industries where all the answers were known and where these products logically should have developed: the stainless steel razor blade, the electric shaver, nonwoven fabrics, epoxy adhesives, the Volkswagen, pipelines, transistors, Dycril printing plates, nylon stockings, Corfam poromeric materials, and latex-based paints.

The great danger is that men "group think" within their own industry about new developments and market potentials. Others often do what they decided couldn't be done. No industry really remains the closed club it thinks it is for very long. The greatest competitive threat lies outside the industry's old-guard group. When the old guard has thought together about its problems too long it finds it impossible to inject radically new points of view. Others, outside the industry, do what couldn't be done and do it profitably.

What Are the Strategic Levels of Attack on New Technology?

Next, one must ask: How little is too little? In other words, what is the difference between subcritical and strategic levels of attack? This is one of the most neglected and least understood aspects of the management of technology.

If you are going to seriously explore any new area of technology there is a level of effort below which the probability of developing anything significant is so poor that experience says the effort isn't worthwhile. In other words when someone plans to schedule some work on a new technology, he should take a second look at the state of the art and arrive at some measure of the magnitude of the job that should be done if it's to be done properly. Then he should raise the question as to whether or not it's worthwhile to do anything less. Subcritical levels of attack have very poor productivity.

It's just another way of saying that if a job is worth doing, it is worth doing well. When you are tackling new technology it's an all-or-nothing sort of thing. A strategic level of attack is productive, a subcritical level of attack is a waste of time.

Look at this in a different way: What applies to one company's programs applies to another company's programs. When you can identify an area of technology that is being explored at a subcritical level by a competitor who doesn't recognize the subcritical aspect of his attack, you have identified an area where you have the probable competitive advantage of attacking that area of technology at a strategic level.

For example, the paint industry has done nothing significant over recent years—the same years when Du Pont developed fast-drying lacquers, General Electric developed alkyd resins, and Dow developed latex-based paints. None of these companies were in the surface-coating business, but by making an attack on a problem at a strategic level they achieved leadership positions. The largest corporations in the photographic industry failed to make a significant attack on the problem of an instantaneous development process for a positive print. Polaroid developed a profitable product by making an all-out effort rather than approaching the problem as just another project.

Take a look at programs that competitors are supporting at subcritical levels to detect and define potentially profitable new technology. Do well what they're doing poorly.

What Opportunities Does Technological Forecasting Highlight?

Most admit that Jules Verne's creations and Victor Appleton's Tom Swift did a pretty good job of outlining the present areas of significant technology long before commercial opportunities were recognized. Verne's oceanographic exploration vehicles and Tom Swift's artificial diamonds are relatively recent commercial realities. Yet most companies still overlook the contributions of technological forecasting in highlighting targets for technology. Some companies, however, do make good use of technological forecasting to pinpoint directions for further exploration.

One of the most effective ways of implementing a program of technological forecasting is to organize a panel of entrepreneurially oriented individuals—that is, bring together the idea men both from inside and outside the company. The purpose of the panel is to draw together all the available sources of information, the output of such sources as basic science investigations, demand analysis, and business conditions projections, and then to establish some directions for worthwhile work. The panel's most important function is not that of making exhaustive critical appraisals but rather that of synthesizing systems with different technologies. An interdisciplinary regrouping will reveal opportunities. One of the important ingredients is a best guess about probable shifts from present to future demands.

In looking backward one can recognize dramatic changes, but looking forward is more profitable. The things one takes for granted may be subjects for research by more imaginative men. The copper producers felt secure with their markets until someone outside the industry asked the question: Is there a better way to conduct electricity?

Some scientists and engineers think they have indeed found a better way. Sodium conducts as much current as copper, which costs six times more money. One kilogram of sodium will conduct as much current as 3.25 kilograms of copper.

Years ago Union Carbide's Linde Division did some technological forecasting, and synthetic sapphires tailor-made for specific applications were the result. A General Electric group in Santa Barbara California has as its assignment the development of profiles of new ways of living and doing business 25 years from now. Technological forecasting can be a powerful tool in detecting and defining targets for technology. G.E.'s synthetic diamonds turned Tom Swift's dream into reality; 3M and others have created a whole new market for synthetic grass for indoor and outdoor use. Imagineering produces profits.

What Are Our Capabilities?

Another good question to ask is: What are the company's capabilities? There's danger of losing sight of the real range of a company's capability spectrum by overidentification of these capabilities with a specific product. Company after company has been a victim of this. A company's capabilities have more latitude than the limited application of these capabilities at a particular time.

Focus thinking on the real range of your capability spectrum. Regard the application of these capabilities as transitory. Live and grow as a company by building flexibility into your thinking. Those who just identify company capabilities with some specific utility find that the company is in trouble when the need for that utility disappears.

Now take a look at some specific cases. Over the years there have been a great many manufacturers of household thermostats. Most of the companies that made these thermostats are no longer heard of. On the other hand, those with a broader perspective capitalized on the capabilities called for in the design and development of thermostats. For example, thinking of the thermostat as a temperature sensor, anticipator, indicator, programmer, and controller, Honeywell recognized that its range of capability extended from instrument technology to computer technology to medical equipment technology.

It has taken many companies in the watch business a long time to realize that their operations were suffering from too great an identification with a specific product. Because they didn't recognize that they were in the precision-instrument business they didn't recognize their potential for precision-product innovation. They weren't able to see beyond their current product line. After Bulova made the only significant innovation in the watch industry in over a hundred years, it took a good look at its capabilities. The new look proved profitable; now Bulova makes instruments. The company's real capability was a talent for turning new technology into dollars. The utilization of science and engineering does prove profitable.

What Business Are We In?

Tied to the question "What are our capabilities?" is the question "What business are we in?" The answer to the question, "What do we do?" can be a provocative producer of ideas and information. A company has a much broader business base as a foundation for development than it generally recognizes. For example, Linde Air Products for many years thought of itself as a producer of gases of varying chemical composition. Another look revealed that to develop, produce, and market different gases, the company was in the business of showing people how to use these gases. To do this the company had to know more about how to use them than did its customers. This recognition of one unsuspected capability led to the recognition of yet another—and made possible Linde's development of synthetic sapphires and rubies.

General Tire and Rubber started out as a manufacturer of tire-patching kits. Recognizing that because it was in the tire industry it should obviously have a knowledge of rubber technology changed the whole future of its business. Over the years, there have been over 350 manufacturers of automobile tires. None of those who thought that they were just in the tire business are still operating, let alone those who thought they just made tire patches.

Cincinnati Milacron made milling machines for many years but it was really in the metal-forming and equipment industry. The company did not limit its vision to milling machines, and its products today incorporate electrochemical processes and computer programming equipment. Meanwhile, other companies in the industry make today what they made 25 years ago.

Minnesota Mining and Manufacturing started out as a manufacturer of abrasive papers. Today it's almost a case of you-name-it, they-make-it, all the way from the familiar Scotch tape or Thermofax machine to surgical supplies. Ask 3-M's top people what business they're in and they'll tell you: making money. Why not? It's hard to beat as a profit producer.

What Is Our Real Competition?

The greatest competitive threat lies in a direction from which it is least expected. This threat is in the form of action by companies that didn't know it couldn't be done or didn't know it couldn't be sold. No company and no industry has exclusive rights on perceptiveness or inventiveness. Industries have been revolutionized by outsiders.

Yet this same threat can be turned into an opportunity. Put another way, the opportunity is that of taking a fresh look at the business areas others dominate today.

When one company announces it is entering a new business area, a second company has an opportunity to introduce a new technological concept in one of the first company's original areas of business. This has been done in the past and will be done in the future as the result of an aggressive approach to new technology by profit-minded management groups.

A onetime producer of calcium carbide for automobile headlights now has divisions in these areas: chemicals, olefins, plastics, silicones, carbon products, industrial gases, mining and metals, Stellite, consumer products, fibers, fabrics, food products, and nuclear science. The company's name is the Union Carbide Corporation.

A tire company, besides producing tires, manufactures a whole range of rubber products, chemicals, resins, adhesives, flooring, vinyl products, films, shoe products, foam products, metal products, aviation products, electronics products, photo processing equipment, communications satellites, weapons systems, radar equipment, airframe assemblies, lightweight armor, data processing equipment, and undersea warfare systems. The name of the company is the Goodyear Tire & Rubber Company.

One of Goodyear's competitors runs an airline, a television network, and a moving picture complex, among other wide-ranging activities. Its name is The General Tire and Rubber Company and its profits have increased steadily over the years.

Gillette thought it knew its competitors until an entrepreneurially minded manufacturer of garden shears entered the razor blade market and introduced a technological innovation, the stainless steel razor blade. It's important to ask the question: Do we know our competition?

Are We Utilizing Each Product's Potential?

Answers to the question "What else can it do?" often point in the direction of potentially profitable new technology. The company that produced the first bug bomb closed out this product when competition started to build up. Had management asked the right question—"Can a bug bomb do more than kill mosquitos?"—the company would have had a line of profitable new products today. Asking the right question often points to new technology worth exploiting. Asking the right question about bug bombs would have pointed to the potential of aerosols and self-contained power sources.

Some of the important questions to ask are: What is it? How can it be used? Who could use it? When? Where? Why?

The first question is the key to potential product applications. Asking the right question would have highlighted the fact that a bug bomb is a self-contained and portable power-pack. Most products also have other potential applications—if you dig deeply enough to see what they may be.

Is Technological Cross Talk Being Tapped?

Too many companies fail to make full use of the opportunities their technical teams have created. They get good ideas but they don't exhaust the full potential of the many facets of these ideas. They overlook opportunities that competitors can exploit.

A good job of exploiting new technology calls for balanced research in eight areas—basic research, product research, application research, process research, equipment research, market research, consumer research, and management research. Each is important. And the cross talk and feedback among research groups can have a synergistic effect.

For example, basic research may develop liquid crystals or ordered fluids color-sensitive to temperature changes. Such a development has no utility until someone points to a need. Process research, however, may recognize that these ordered fluids are the missing link in a new process being considered. Equipment research, on another occasion, may point to a potential application for a new electrical etching technique. Management research, research into the management process itself, may point to a way of making better use of overall resources.

Wherever scientists and engineers are at work, technology useful to someone else may be developed. During the early days of the transistor, the "noise" the process research people were trying to remove from the transistor resulted in data that led to a whole new area of research and a new generation of thermoelectric materials. Cross talk led to the turning of noise into profit dollars. Cross talk can only be effective when the research spectrum is balanced—when scientists and engineers are looking in all directions all the time.

The ultimate end of new technology is its effective utilization. If research efforts are balanced in all important areas and talked over by all concerned, attention will be called to important new technology that might otherwise be overlooked by those who confine their thinking to their own parochial areas of application.

Do Fads and Fashions Point to Profits or Pitfalls?

Other good questions to ask are: What are others doing? Can we capitalize on fads and fashions by recognizing and then avoiding the pitfalls they present? Doing what others are doing just because they are doing it may turn out to be a bad decision. Others can be wrong. And even when they're right, what's right for them may be wrong for us.

There have been fads and fashions in research and engineering, too. It's easy to fall into the trap of doing something just because others are doing it. We read about new things in the newspapers, technical publications, and popular periodicals and we hear about them at technical meetings and even out on the golf course. Because everyone else is exploring a new area of technology it's easy to jump to the conclusion that our company should do some exploratory work in this area, too. The experience of the past warns us to use extra caution. Here's why.

1. Just because the government is granting a great many contracts in one area of technology, say magnetohydrodynamics, doesn't mean that this will be a profitable area for every company. Because of government contracts it may be impossible to establish proprietary positions as a basis for long-range profits.

2. Just because there is a market for some kind of new technology, say monolithic circuitry, doesn't mean that the technical people in

every company have even the remotest contribution to make to it. They may, however, have some excellent ideas about some other worthwhile things in other areas.

3. Just because everyone else may be working in a particular area of technology, say oceanography, doesn't mean that that area spells opportunity for your company. When everyone is thinking about the same thing, the profitability of a program is likely to be diluted and perhaps even eliminated.

4. Just because older established ways of doing something can be improved by scientific methods doesn't mean that doing so will necessarily be profitable. For example, just because the silk-screen printing process can be improved is no guarantee of an adequate return on the necessary investment.

5. Just because one can do something big, say plan a trip to the moon or bore a hole into the center of the earth, doesn't mean it's the most worthwhile way to spend your company's money.

6. Just because a company may spread its technical team over every possible project in its industry doesn't guarantee effective programs in any of the target areas. Having every man on the technical team spend one day a week on a maximum number of different projects would be the most disastrous thing that could be done.

7. Just because a project provides good publicity doesn't insure long-term profitability. Almost anything new and different gets publicity. Profits are harder to get. It's easy to get attention; the thing to get is results.

8. Just because you can publish a paper doesn't prove you can produce profits. There is a negative correlation between publishing and profiting from technical programs.

The payoff in technical programming has never come from fashionability. It's based on selectivity. It's difficult to maintain a discriminating attitude in the face of fads and fashions but doing so has proved profitable.

Knowledge about what others are doing, however, can be useful in detecting and defining new technology. Such information may sound a warning whistle. The chairman of the board of a major chemical company and a man in charge of his company's technical programs, made this comment: "Whenever I hear that the XYZ Company is committing funds for research in a particular area of technology, I know it's not worth our giving any further thought to that particular area of technology. That company has been 100 percent successful in investing its money in the development of the wrong technology, time and time again." He used this knowledge of what others were doing to tell him what not to do.

What Opportunities Are Presented by Our Industry Posture?

Still another good question to ask is: What company image are our customers buying? Every company is identified with a particular posture within its industry. A company may be recognized as the one that does all the new and different things. Another company may be identified as the one that specializes in particular products. A third may be thought of as being in a position of leadership with respect to distribution and service facilities. Still other companies are identified as followers or laggards.

A company's industry posture provides opportunities for management to do some things to better advantage than others. For example, IBM occupies a position of leadership in computer technology and can pioneer new products with a greater assurance of acceptance than other companies, particularly those that have long been laggards in the data processing industry. A progressive company's customers will be companies that have capitalized on innovation and know how to put new products to good use as soon as they are available. A company's industry posture provides guidelines to put to use in detecting and defining new technology.

A review of company objectives may suggest areas for exploration that might have been overlooked or not recognized as open territory for product development. The president of Borden Incorporated told a group of New York security analysts that: "No area of growth is too far afield to explore; no area of past growth is too traditional to cling to if it loses its promise. Our aim is to develop a higher degree of flexibility, adaptability, and resourcefulness to seek out and exploit greater opportunities wherever they may exist." When objectives are set forth in a broad framework like this, research and engineering people can look in all directions for opportunities. Objectives as stated by any management group are basic guidelines for defining and detecting new technology.

It's important that everyone in the technical organization be made aware of the things that are of interest to management. At the same time management must be made aware of areas of new technology that suggest some restructuring of corporate objectives. Cross talk between management, scientists, and engineers must be continuous. It's critical to corporate success.

An organization's personnel is continually changing. Organizational fluidity makes it necessary to be sure that the newer scientists and engineers, and other corporate newcomers are adequately informed about matters of mutual interest. It's a big job and one that is never finished. Developing a greater awareness of corporate objectives on the part of scientists and engineers produces profit dollars.

The Decision-making Dilemma

These ten guidelines for detecting and defining potentially profitable technology reflect a synthesis of the experience of companies that have proved they know how to plan profitable programs. These guidelines set the stage for further thinking. They focus attention on effective action and its end product—results measurable in profit dollars.

Two groups of managers must share responsibility for the success of this entrepreneurial activity. Top management's action determines overall corporate objectives. Managers of technical programs must aggressively establish beachheads in areas of technology related to corporate objectives. Continuing cross talk is critically important because it must also play an active role in the restructuring of corporate goals.

In making decisions about the utilization of technology two things should be kept in mind.

First, the accelerated tempo of technological development responding to competitive forces has greatly compressed the interval between the long-range plan and its implementation. You just do things faster when somebody else is competing with you for the same carrot on the end of a stick. This simple truth applies to the plans of individuals, corporations, and nations. A single company doesn't decide how fast a race must be run in developing new technology; competition sets the tempo for technological advance.

Second, once top management decides that it has the capacity and the willingness to assume risk in capitalizing on new technology, the detecting and defining of potentially profitable new technology must be made the responsibility of its technical people. No one else is qualified to make critical decisions with regard to new technology. In fact, one might hope that a competitor's nontechnical people are doing the deciding with respect to new technology. Permitting nontechnical people to make technical decisions has cost companies their corporate lives. The track record points to the fact that it's relatively easy to win the race if competitors provide you with this kind of advantage.

Learning to Live with Change

Today's managers must learn to live with change. Tomorrow's approach to the utilization of technology won't be solved by yesterday's management methods. Sound administration must be based on more than reference to the guidelines of the past. One gets a head start by putting experience to work, but a forward look is the basis of leadership. Management's approach must be eclectic as well as pragmatic. A borrowing of the best of past and present practices coupled with innovative action in administering corporate affairs is the source of success at the program level as well as at the policy level.

15

Integrating Technology and Markets

THE commercial development function steers the new product development program. Optimum results are achieved when the steering is done by men who can assess both the technical and economic aspects of proposed new products.

Corporations that have research, engineering, and commercial development groups are ideally structured. The relative roles of these functional relationships are shown in Exhibit 3.

The scientist's function in the research organization is the detection, classification, and organization of facts, laws, and hypotheses relating to phenomena, materials, and the arts. The engineer's function is to translate these facts, laws, and hypotheses into new products or improved products. The commercial development function orients product concepts to commercial opportunities and attempts to fully develop them and capitalize on them.

Role of the Commercial Development Group

The commercial development group occupies a pivotal position in development programs because of its close relationship to the business scene. The work of this group encompasses the following activities:

Search for new product ideas
Development of industry growth trends (and decline trends, too)

Business conditions analysis
Consumer preference and demand studies
Appraisals of product performance
Analysis of product lines and product mix
Definition of potentially profitable product concepts
Recommendations on the relative commercial feasibility of proposed
    research and engineering programs and new product concepts
Coordination of business development programs
Surveys of various types
Consultation services for other divisions
Periodic reevaluation of programs and projections
Formulation of business development programs

These are broad responsibilities. Each is vitally important in planning for future growth and in achieving growth objectives.

Product- and Market-oriented Evaluation

At one extreme, the company has an idea and wants to know its worth. At the opposite extreme, the company wants to know what opportunities exist for new products that would fill an unsatisfied need.

In the first case, where the company has an idea, the evaluation process is product-oriented. In the second case, evaluation is market-oriented.

Product-oriented evaluations generally present the most perplexing problems because of pressure for prompt and affirmative action. Those

Exhibit 3. Developing business opportunities, functional analysis.

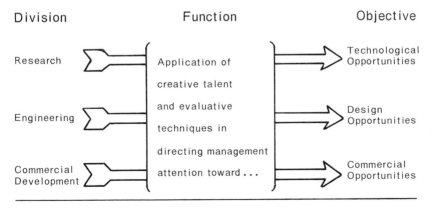

who present new ideas generally consider themselves greatly misused if they receive anything short of overwhelming endorsement.

Market-oriented evaluations may be even more important to the corporation. Since no personal interests are involved, pressure is rarely exerted. Regardless of the fact that evaluation of opportunities extends to the two extremes represented by product- and market-oriented evaluation programs, both must fit into overall corporate objectives—they must be company-oriented as well.

Orienting Objectives

The commercial development group can aid substantially in establishing properly oriented programs. When engineers and research scientists know the objectives management has set, they know what is expected and can work toward these goals. Too often, management's objectives are not known because management itself has not formulated any objectives.

Executives may fall into the habit of citing objectives to excuse their position, whether it's positive or negative. It's easy to turn down a proposal because it's not in line with objectives. At the same time, executives who justify their actions by ready reference to objectives are often unable to explain the significance of these objectives.

Incorporation of new products into the corporation's product portfolio calls for

Determination of objectives
Detection of ideas and markets
Definition of commercial potentials
Decision making
Direction of development programs

Responsibility for these five functions must be fixed. For effective operations, these activities should be centralized in a group given full responsibility for commercial development programs.

Determination of Objectives

Objectives represent goals to be achieved in a specified time period and are the basis of planning. Some executives consider objectives highly confidential. Goals serve no purpose unless they are known to everyone directly or indirectly concerned with their achievement. Much of the confusion in planning is directly traceable to the fact that goals are not known and understood.

Setting up objectives takes time and skill, as does reevaluating them. As new opportunities arise, old objectives should be appraised and, when necessary, restated in accordance with changed conditions.

Detection of Ideas and Markets

The commercial development group develops inside and outside sources to draw on in developing ideas and market information— thereby enlarging the total effectiveness of the corporation's efforts.

The group is then in a position to meet with research scientists, engineers, and others to help them understand the commercial significance of programs. Information about related developments having a direct bearing on specific programs is supplied and market requirements interpreted.

Given full responsibility for the development of new business, the commercial development group acts independently in using outside research, engineering, and marketing services where necessary. This is desirable for a number of reasons. Research, engineering, and marketing may not be staffed or have time to take on additional assignments.

For the long-run best interests of the company, exploratory programs should not be blocked by such factors—nor should the commercial development group have the authority to compel compliance with their wishes. They should, however, be free to act independently. This freedom will tend to exert a corrective effect where necessary. The real objective is to keep programs moving.

Definition of Commercial Potentials

A summary of the commercial potential of ideas and market opportunities provides the basis for measuring their relative value. Management rarely has resources available sufficient to take advantage of every opportunity presented. The best must be selected. Definition of commercial potentials is a positioning process, or clarification of ideas and concepts, management acceptability, patentability, and technical-economic evaluation.

The primary responsibility of the commercial development division is the definition of commercial opportunities, with full responsibility for their development. Ideas and concepts are examined for the purpose of measuring their commercial potential, and formal presentations are made to management.

To do this most effectively, members of the commercial development group should have an intimate acquaintance with top management thinking and thereby be able to recognize management's need for additional background data and initiate studies without waiting for management to specifically request them. While management in certain instances may request special studies, it should be a recognized responsibility of the commercial development division to initiate studies and surveys as quickly as its people see the need for it.

In this respect, the commercial development division functions as a management services group. This relationship to top management is vitally essential to successful performance of the functions of the division. At all times, the commercial development division must be thoroughly informed and conversant with business activities inside and outside the corporation. Its own work should reflect leadership in business thinking.

As research reveals technological opportunities and engineering suggests design opportunities, commercial development should point to commercial opportunities. At the same time, it should integrate all three into programs for formal presentation to management, accompanied by specific recommendations for executive action.

1. *Clarification of ideas and concepts.* Evaluation of a new idea depends on a clear statement of the idea itself in a form understandable to those who may be able to point out strengths and weaknesses. Opportunities for new products growing out of detectable market needs must be defined in very much the same way. Statements dealing with the scope of the product concept link a descriptive title to a brief resume of the sponsor's thoughts and answer such questions as: What does the idea contribute by way of new function, improved function, or lowered costs? How is this accomplished? Why is this done in this particular manner? What alternative methods exist? Why was the proposed method selected?

2. *Establishing acceptability to management.* Top management should review proposed product development programs prior to initiating any major undertaking. Ideas that do not fit management's interests are removed from further consideration at this point. Since further activity on such programs wastes resources available for product development, any major effort should be deferred until an effective presentation can be prepared to establish management approval and support.

Management reaction to any new product proposal is motivated by a number of factors, among which are the business outlook, corporate objectives, timing, and individual likes and dislikes. All have an important bearing on the general acceptability of ideas for new products. This is why an intimate familiarity with management thinking can be put to good use by the commercial development division. Effective presentations will reflect a recognition of what has motivated past action by management.

3. *Resolving patentability.* Controlling patents and licensing agreements should be identified and their scope and limitations established. This is essential to find out what proprietary interests can be acquired in the new idea and what steps are necessary to secure rights to permit commercial development.

New ideas, particularly those coming from outside, should not be submitted to technical groups until this step is completed. The commercial development group can thus prevent premature disclosure to the technical organization and avoid unwarranted disclosure of company thinking about new products. Work conducted in the course of development programs may parallel that suggested by proposed ideas. Where this is the case, it is essential to establish proof of this fact prior to entering into any negotiations that include the company's scientists and engineers. Disclosure of the commercial feasibility of proposed ideas seriously complicates negotiations for their acquisition.

One important question to be resolved by the commercial development division is whether or not patentability is essential to commercial success. When it is essential, the question is: Can the product or process be patented? This analysis is best centralized in the commercial development division, where dollar signs can be attached to the various factors in decision making.

4. *Evaluation of technical-economic factors.* In defining proposed programs, the group must examine technical and economic factors. Each has a direct bearing on the other. The object is to examine an idea in the light of available knowledge so that time and money will be spent only on programs that are relatively good risks. As evidence bearing on the relative commercial feasibility of ideas is brought into focus, product programs can be directed into the most productive channels.

Technical-economic investigations should explore each of the following areas:

Outlook for the industry identified with the proposed product
Important features of the proposed product
Effect of patents and licenses on introduction of the product
Effect of a proposed product on relationships growing out of products currently offered
Market for the product
Distribution for the product
Competition to be anticipated
Estimated costs and potential profits
Threat presented by future technological development

In the development of resource material for decision making, it should be remembered that the factual information desired usually is not available; indeed in most instances it does not exist. This is often overlooked in efforts to prepare reports that are "loaded" with factual data. In case after case, overzealousness in a search for facts has resulted in the rejection of the opinions and observations of well-informed men. The irony is that their comments, in the long run, are worth far more than data.

Day-to-day programs can be guided by decisions based on facts. Programming for the future, however, must be based on a different type of guidance. Farsighted business planning calls for vision—not historical facts. This is the difference between a market study and a study of market opportunities.

Those responsible for long-range planning should insist on evaluation in the light of the conditions that will exist as these programs unfold rather than in the light of current conditions. There is some basis for suggesting to the investigator that he forget the past entirely, that he forget facts, that instead he seek out men who have intuition, discernment, analysis, and judgment. Observations of such men are worth more than files full of data.

Such an approach does not reduce the investigator's workload, for it is more difficult to locate such individuals than to locate pertinent data. Perhaps the reason reports are so frequently weighed down with data is that it is easier to find data than men who see ahead.

Picking men of vision means picking the men who have the ability to project their thinking into the future and call the turns most of the time. These are some of the characteristics they have in common: a naturally questioning approach to all matters coming within their view, acute powers of observation, an ability to concentrate on problems, and an ability to associate ideas and facts in new relationships—the key to projecting thinking forward with a high degree of accuracy.

It is doubtful that anyone has developed a reliable formula for selecting men who have the ability to take leadership positions in long-range thinking and planning. The best guide in selecting such individuals is past performance.

Decision Making
The commercial development group does not make final decisions. Data is digested for management review and decision since management cannot find time to review and analyze all the facts that must enter into decision making. The commercial development group has

the responsibility of preparing program presentations for management in a way that will minimize demands on management time. Therefore, some decisions must be made by the commercial development group— decisions that may have a far-reaching significance. For this reason, management must have full confidence in the group's ability.

With the help of the group, management should establish objectives and criteria for future programs to increase the group's effectiveness. Formulas, profiles, ratings, and other systems have been devised to evaluate proposed programs, but it can be seriously questioned whether these systems work. A review of a number of programs where rating systems are reported to have been used suggests that at best they played only a minor role.

Some rating systems have been adopted with great enthusiasm, only to be set aside when it appeared they were not tailored to the job. Later, the system was dusted off, the facts put in place, and the rating system revised to substantiate the program adopted.

In these cases, the actual evaluation system appears to grow out of the individual programs. The evaluation, rather than proceeding from the general to the specific, has begun with consideration of the specific problem and gone on from there. This is particularly significant because it indicates that danger lurks in the shadow of any generalized plan for evaluating programs.

Another common problem associated with program evaluation is tied to the practice of basing decisions on the relation between returns (sales less costs) and total investment in the project. Such a basis of evaluation neglects any consideration of the time value of money. Recognition of the association between investment of funds and existence of alternative investment opportunities, with associated rates of return, is essential. When sizable sums are involved, the time value of money is appreciable and becomes an important element in evaluating programs.

Direction of Development Programs

Responsibility for coordinating and directing development programs should be fixed and centralized. Until new programs can be assigned to one of the operating divisions, the development group is in the best position to give close attention.

Even in the best-planned programs, problems will arise in the initial stages that demand top management attention. The commercial development group can bring problems to the attention of management and supply management with data needed in decision making.

Organization of the Development Group

The commercial development division should be organized so as to permit problems and proposals to receive individual attention and at the same time be subject to expert review where necessary. A most effective way of achieving this is by assigning individual programs to project supervisors and then making the services of specialists available to them through an organization structure such as that shown in Exhibit 4.

The project supervisor is given complete charge of specific assignments. His staff complement is determined by assignment requirements, and the services of the marketing, product, and economic advisory groups are made available. He is permitted to exercise his own discretion in the use he makes of these services.

Although the project supervisor is responsible for the completed assignment, either the project director or the executive officer may ask members of the economics, marketing, or product staff to review reports and comment. This double check assures that all programs are analyzed in breadth and depth.

The staff supervisors are responsible for developing thorough knowledge and background in their respective areas. Their training and experience should therefore reflect specialization and competence. While project supervisors are responsible for assigned projects, staff supervisors are responsible for calling to management's attention specific matters of significance that are developing within their respective areas.

The economic analysis supervisor is responsible for keeping management informed of impending changes in business conditions. Every

Exhibit 4. Commercial development department organization.

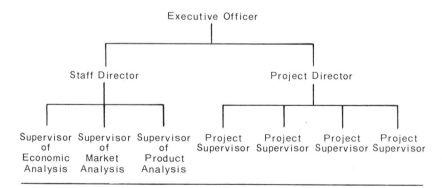

available resource should be exhausted in fulfilling this responsibility. Specific functions assigned fit into four categories: (1) definition of industry trends, (2) business conditions analysis, (3) development of corporate acquisition programs, (4) initiation of business development programs.

The last two responsibilities are shared with market and product supervisors. Staff members in each area should concentrate part of their effort in a search for new opportunities for potentially profitable new business or desirable acquisitions.

The market analysis supervisor is responsible for developing market information. Project supervisors and management both need a source to which they can turn for competent counsel in this highly important area of specialization. The market analysis supervisor is responsible for consumer preference and demand studies, development of corporate acquisition programs, initiation of business development programs. Exercising this responsibility entails full use of outside sources of information in conjunction with work of an adequately staffed market analysis group reporting directly to the market analysis supervisor.

The product analysis supervisor is principally concerned with physical products and their relationships. His activities fall into six broad areas: a search for new product ideas, appraisals of product performance, analysis of product lines and product mix, definition of potentially profitable products, development of corporate acquisition programs, initiation of business development programs.

The product analysis supervisor should have a high degree of technical competence and his staff a wide range of technical competence. To operate effectively, the commercial development division must be able to evaluate the significance of new technology.

The staff director has an administrative responsibility and a somewhat broader function in counseling management and members of the project group. From an administrative position, the staff director is responsible for the professional competence of the groups concerned with economic, market, and product analysis and their effectiveness in completing assignments as needed. In his broader function, acting as counsel to management, he has six areas of responsibility: evaluation of the relative commercial feasibility of proposed research and engineering programs and new product concepts, coordination of business development programs, surveys, consultation services, development of corporate acquisition programs, initiation of business development programs.

Individual assistance requested from the three staff supervisors is provided directly. These extremely broad duties place the staff director in the position of counsel to management on matters within his purview.

The executive officer of the commercial development department has full responsibility for all activities, maintaining operations at a level commensurate with the total company effort and making certain that the department's potential contributions are fully utilized. This is a continuing counseling responsibility in itself.

Commercial development is a management service. Research and engineering managers need reliable commercial counsel to operate effectively. Top management needs assistance of unquestioned reliability. To insure a communications pattern that adequately informs, interprets, and advises, commercial "intelligence" should be centralized.

16

Research for Results

MISUNDERSTANDING of the research function probably accounts for more lost dollars during product development than any other single factor. Frequently what is really meant by research is not understood, nor is it understood how to use research effectively. Huge amounts of money are spent every year on research but only a fraction of the sum results in worthwhile output.

The managements of too many companies have been more concerned with large research appropriations than with the need for a penetrating analysis of research operations. Research is not product development, yet in recent years research departments in many companies have been sidetracked by product development assignments. This has been the result of management decree. In other instances it reflects empire building.

As an immediate consequence of this increase in the scope of research activities, essential research programs have been pushed aside in favor of more immediate production problems. Research staffs are usually competent in handling a wide range of assignments that could and should be handled by others. This competence has proved costly when it has resulted in diversion of research talent on nontechnical assignments.

Effective research administration calls for an understanding of this vitally important phase of business activity. A complete understanding comes only through experience resulting from actual administration of research programs. Practical experience is made much more profitable when time is set aside for review and analysis of the administrative process of research management.

Research Objectives

Research points the way to new business opportunities—new products, new processes, and lowered costs. Once these opportunities are revealed, engineers should take over the job of developing the most promising. This leaves the research group free for further exploratory studies. If this policy is not followed, the exploratory studies stop because there is no time for them. New ideas cease to flow and stagnation sets in.

The function of industrial research is to develop new knowledge and understanding—

To insure that the corporation will continue to operate in areas of growing business activity and profit potential.

To make the best possible use of corporation resources such as raw materials, technical specialties, and management talent.

To utilize available markets adequately.

To insure steadily increasing and stable profits.

To contribute to the corporation's ability to accept social and humanitarian responsibilities.

New technology and accumulated scientific knowledge must be scrutinized constantly in an atmosphere of changing needs to find new and potentially usable product concepts. At the same time, new skills and techniques must be developed as needed to enlarge the scope and effectiveness of the research process. Research continually freshens product thinking and stimulates product development activities. It provides new concepts, principles, and technical supporting data. These fruits of research form the basis of product development.

Profits from Research

Difficulty will always be encountered in making every research program pay off. An attempt to do so would seriously cripple research efforts. From a practical business position, however, projects must be reviewed periodically and those projects terminated that are obviously not heading in directions of significance to the corporation.

Some businessmen—and some scientists, too—have stated that research never results in losses. This is sheer nonsense. While research programs may produce new knowledge, unless it represents useful knowledge, it will not produce new income. Shareholders look for increased equity and dividends. Soundly administered research makes a major contribution and is a profitable investment.

There is something radically wrong with research programs that do not lead to new income. A failure to produce returns reflects on the research manager. Research is a basic business function. It can be mismanaged like any other business activity with resulting losses to the corporation, or it can be effectively administered and produce profits obtainable in no other way.

Research Spending

Management must approve research appropriations—a difficult job. Any good research group can think up ways to spend money faster than it can be accumulated. This is a sign of healthy, active research thinking.

A research group should indicate areas that it thinks might prove profitable to the company. It is up to management to determine how much of the overall program it is feasible to tackle. This decision must take into consideration available funds and management's growth objectives. Judgment should replace reliance on statistical percentages.

Wisdom in establishing research programs depends to a large degree on the ability to answer—

1. How much are competitors spending on research?
2. How is research productivity related to research appropriations?
3. How much would it cost to make effective use of research results?
4. How much can the corporation afford to appropriate for growth?

Competitor activity. In answering the first question, management should be guided by appraisals of competitive situations within individual industries. An appraisal of competitive research activity will reveal the size of programs that must be undertaken to maintain or improve an industry position. If analysis discloses extensive research activity by competitors, these programs must be offset to maintain the present industry position. In attempting to offset such programs, a calculated risk arises. It is impossible to be certain that contemplated programs will balance out those of competitors.

Research productivity. Accuracy in answering the second question comes with experience. There is no precise way of determining the relationship of output to expenditures. Companies with long-established research programs can project past experience to establish estimates. However, no two research programs have the same output. Research productivity depends on many factors. The selection of projects, the planning of investigational programs, and the staffing of these programs determine productivity. Multiple-project programs will allow performance averaging.

Cost of using research results. Not only is it necessary to estimate the cost of productive research programs, but it is equally important to know how much it will cost to turn research results into commercially feasible projects. Timing is a cost factor, too. Rarely can research results be tabled or shelved until resources are available for their application. Competition will not permit this. Research results that are put on the shelf are usually forfeited to competitors.

Management must maintain a sensitivity to competitive conditions in funding research programs. Some management groups will be faster to act than others. In part, this reflects management's receptiveness to new ideas as well as its responsiveness to the added demands on executive time that necessarily accompany any new undertaking.

Size of investment. Another part of the overall picture is identified with the availability of funds for corporate expansion. There is always an upper limit to the amount of money that can be diverted from current income for investment in the future. An evaluation of the upper limit of funds that will be available in future years for research and the commercial development of new products provides a basis for establishing research budgets. These budgets must effectively be in balance with funds available for turning research results into products.

There is a practical limit to the size of research programs that corporations can undertake. Growth costs money. Competitive research activity and growth objectives indicate the magnitude of research programs that may be necessary. Follow-through on commercial products incorporating results of the research is part of the total cost of growth. Research is useless unless it results in profitable products. Commercial development competence is inseparably linked to the ultimate achievement of growth objectives.

Profitable Research Projects

The determination of areas of new knowledge that may prove profitable is the starting point in project development. Broad areas in the sciences should be explored to uncover additional opportunities for applying what is already known. New technologies frequently reveal untapped commercial opportunities.

The corporation's products should be analyzed as a basis for developing research programs. Products rarely provide optimum performance. Few materials, principles, or systems are applied at maximum effectiveness. Analysis of consumer needs discloses subjects for research investigations.

In analyzing products four questions are pertinent:

1. In what ways do specific products fall short of the consumer's ideal?
2. What manufacturing limitations prevent production of this ideal product?
3. What technical limits are imposed on laboratory models of the ideal product?
4. What theoretical limits exist?

Answers to each of these questions reveal areas where knowledge can be put to good use by the corporation.

Before any research is attempted to develop new knowledge, an effort should be made to locate the answers to pertinent questions on the basis of existing knowledge. A survey should be conducted to identify investigations under way by other research groups that might result in pertinent information for the problem at hand.

A requirement for research is indicated when existing knowledge falls short of needs. The priority of needs is established by evaluating the probable outcome of research, projected returns from research efforts, and associated costs of research investigations.

Organization of Research Programs

Discussions of organization structure have the common fault of being either so specific or so general that they are useless. Both result from the failure to focus attention on functional interrelationships essential to the accomplishment of organization objectives.

Accomplishment of objectives requires that certain functions be performed. Relatively clear-cut relationships between objectives and functions begin to cloud up as soon as the staffing process commences.

Rarely, if ever, can individuals be found who are tailored to the job. Compromises must be made as the best men available are selected. Jobs are tailored to the knowledge, judgment, experience, and innate ability of the men chosen. It is impossible to anticipate the full impact of the men on the job. Yet without this knowledge, the usefulness of an existing organization cannot be appraised. This limitation necessitates the creation of a model to provide a framework for reference.

The organization structure shown in Exhibit 5 serves as a starting point to establish a new research group and provides a basis for auditing the operations of existing research programs. If research is to be effective, those engaged in research pursuits must be freed from administrative details. Implementing this concept is the starting point in the development of the research organization.

The successful research organization is built around the functions of the administrative director and the scientific director. In smaller research groups, one man may assume both roles.

Few companies will be fortunate enough to find individuals who are competent scientists as well as capable administrators. It is more probable that in the smaller company it will be necessary to make a compromise between a good scientist and poor administrator on the one hand and poor scientist and capable administrator on the other. Where compromise is necessitated by the scale of operations, the better scientist should be chosen. Without the competent scientist there can be no research. As the organization grows, administrative

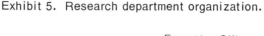

Exhibit 5. Research department organization.

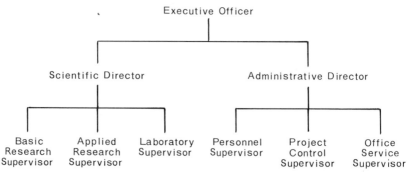

talent can be added. Programs capable of supporting larger organizations can take advantage of the added operating effectiveness resulting from a separation of administrative and scientific functions.

The Administrative Function

The administrative director's role fits a relatively familiar pattern. He is responsible for business relationships in the research organization. His activities can be broken down into three general areas of supervisory responsibility. He is responsible for planning, organizing, and controlling research activities. In carrying out these responsibilities, the administrative director may require the assistance of a project control supervisor, a personnel supervisor, and an office service supervisor.

The project control supervisor is responsible for the development of work schedules for new programs to be undertaken. It is also his responsibility to relate actual performance to established schedules once programs are under way.

New programs must be broken down into manpower and facilities requirements and compared with available supplies of each resource. Based on this analysis, time schedules can be established that are compatible with the men, money, and physical tools available for the project.

The project control supervisor must rely on the advice of those who actually execute programs for the information that goes into making up schedules. He should not attempt to act as an expert in any area of technical specialization. He simply takes facts as they are presented to him and arranges them into objective and realistic programs in terms of dollars and time.

The second major responsibility of the project control supervisor is that of revising schedules as individual projects either lead or lag behind the original estimates. Schedules should always present up-to-the-minute projections of the latest probable course of the development of projects under way. Once project schedules are initially established, management should no longer need to concern itself with a review of these schedules. It should be sufficient to review periodic reports issued by the project control supervisor detailing changes in these original schedules. These changes point up areas requiring further administrative attention. Revised schedules reveal to the research executive the degree to which corporate objectives are being achieved in accordance with established management expectations.

The personnel supervisor is responsible for recruitment and placement of all personnel in the research organization. Final selection of candidates for positions is made by individual supervisors responsible for the area of operations to which new personnel are assigned. The personnel supervisor insures that sources of competent research personnel are tapped. Prospective candidates for positions are screened so that only those individuals reflecting the greatest potential value are referred to key members for consideration. Once new members of the research organization are selected and report for work, the personnel supervisor conducts indoctrination programs.

The personnel supervisor is responsible for the establishment of essential personnel functions in the research organization. This includes responsibility for programs designed to develop professional abilities and capacities.

The office services supervisor has broad responsibilities. Maintenance of the physical plant, management of nontechnical facilities and supplies and services fall within the scope of his activities. Providing for a secretarial staff, report preparation facilities, record maintenance, library services, and related functions essential to the smooth working of a research organization is also his responsibility.

The overall philosophy of the administrative director's role is that of absorbing all functions that are not inseparably tied to the work of the research investigator. This means the research worker's time can be concentrated on the scientific phases of programs to be accomplished. This not only places administrative matters in competent hands but at the same time reduces the diversion of both scarce and valuable research manpower.

To achieve optimum output from research programs, separation of administrative and scientific activities is essential. This organizational practice reflects a pronounced trend in current practices in administering technical programs.

The Scientific Function

The scientific director is responsible for the effective execution of all technical phases of a research program. He is responsible for the development and acquisition of technical personnel and tools necessary to implement these programs.

Objectives and specific program areas are established by the executive officer in charge of research. This is done with the approval of other members of the top management group. In the establishment of these programs, the scientific director should play a particularly important role. As senior scientist closely associated with the individual research programs, he is in a position to be particularly perceptive where significant developments are concerned.

Worthwhile new ideas and concepts are revealed by the work of the research investigator closest to the problem being studied. Unless channels of communication are maintained so that this thinking can flow upward, research programs will be relatively unproductive.

Once ideas have been generated and programs approved, it is the scientific director's primary responsibility to apply the latest knowledge, skills, and facilities in implementing these programs. The scientific function can be further subdivided into areas of responsibility assigned to the applied research supervisor, the basic research supervisor, and the laboratory supervisor.

The applied research supervisor is responsible for the execution of programs that relate directly to the company's products—those in the catalog and those planned for the immediate future. What differentiates applied research from basic research is that applied research is influenced to a very large degree by specific product requirements. This is sufficient to justify the separation of applied research activities from those in the area of basic research.

The basic research supervisor is responsible for programs with the objective of revealing opportunities for new products. Effective basic research requires a certain freedom from day-to-day product responsibilities. This can best be achieved by a distinct functional separation. The element of urgency that frequently attaches itself to applied research may cause these programs to encroach on basic research investigations when this division in overall responsibility is not made.

The laboratory supervisor is responsible for the development of skills and facilities essential in aiding the research investigator. Many of today's scientific tools require highly skilled operators and special laboratory facilities. Newer tools can be expected to accentuate this trend. The laboratory supervisor should cooperate with the individual scientists who constitute the research group in determining requirements for purchasing scientific apparatus. Every effort should be made to anticipate future needs in order that new equipment acquisitions are functioning even before they're needed by the research investigator. Installations frequently involve lengthy training periods that must be completed before any reliability can be attached to the data obtained from a particular piece of apparatus.

The laboratory supervisor is responsible for the development of special equipment required by the research investigator. The objective is to free the scientist from the performance of any tasks that do not make an essential contribution to his work.

The Research Executive

No individual who actually attempts to direct research makes a good research executive. Experienced research executives recognize this. Industrial research is essentially a process of channeling creative thinking into potentially useful and profitable directions. In achieving results that reflect creative thinking, the research director must have the ability to perform three major functions of great importance. He is responsible for the following activities.

Selecting creative thinkers. A good research executive must have the ability to both pick and develop creative thinkers. Everyone has some creative ability but competition demands that the research group comprise the most creative minds available. Past performance is the best criterion of an individual's creative ability, but not the only one. Other criteria, however, are subtle and uncertain. The research executive must match his resources against those of his counterparts in other companies in picking creative people. Without them there can be no research.

Establishing working conditions. He must establish a favorable environment for creative work. Policies, procedures, and facilities must be geared to the creative process. Facilities must be available to the research worker at a minimum of inconvenience on his part. Creative thinking flourishes best under conditions that allow freedom for action. Freedom for action is an absolute must in establishing a favorable environment for creative efforts.

Directing interest. The research executive must stimulate interest in areas of activity that are potentially profitable to the company. This does not preclude the opportunity for independent investigations but it does insure that the major emphasis will lie in areas that appear to have the greatest potential use to the company, which, after all, foots the bill.

Role of the Research Executive

The research executive guides the corporation in the direction of full utilization of new product opportunities as they appear. He does this by interpreting the results of research investigations significant to top management. He must make certain that funds appropriated for research programs are adequate for long-range development of the corporation's product programs. The research executive's responsibilities can be classified in ten major areas.

1. Disclosure to management of new product opportunities revealed by research investigations or suggested by scientific advances. These opportunities serve as a background for deci-

sion making relative to feasibility and marketability of new product concepts.

2. Evaluation of areas of scientific endeavor to isolate opportunities for further work. Evaluation must also include an assessment of the potentials and limitations in such areas.

3. Definition of fields of corporate interest and the stimulation of the recognition of problems in areas of company interest.

4. Selection of the most promising opportunities and the establishment of priorities based on the limitations imposed by time and budgets.

5. Assessment of research proposals in terms of manpower, methods, and facilities required.

6. Implementation of programs.

7. Development of needed technology as rapidly and as efficiently as possible.

8. Reassessment of problems during the course of solving them, with corresponding changes in methods, manpower, and facilities as work proceeds.

9. Abandonment of projects that are not productive or that should be replaced by more promising programs.

10. Cooperation with members of the management team in the application and utilization of new technology.

In discharging these responsibilities, the research executive draws heavily on the resources of his two principal operating executives—the scientific director and the administrative director of the research organization. These men are individually responsible for specific areas of operation. The research executive must maintain a continuing evaluation of the effectiveness of these operations and at the same time develop plans to increase their overall usefulness. In doing this, the research executive may make use of staff assistance for operations research and technical feasibility studies.

Operations Research

One of the major interests of the research executive should be that of research into the research process itself. Investigations of this type can best be handled by staff members in the office of the research executive who specialize in such studies.

These investigators will analyze the more successful research projects, comparing them with less successful programs in an effort to reveal significant operational differences in the handling of the two. The operations research group should construct model organizations and operating procedures in an effort to optimize output from the manpower, money, and facilities devoted to research and development.

Operations research should be a continuing function. Changes are constantly occurring within the research organization and in the general corporate environment in which the research group operates. These changes create opportunities for more effective procedural relationships. Those charged with day-to-day responsibilities usually find it difficult to set aside time for studies designed to improve the efficiency of their own sphere of operations. It is even more difficult for these people to find time to study operations outside their own specific area in order to improve working relationships.

Freed from day-to-day commitments, operations research specialists not only have the time to conduct such studies but also have the opportunity to acquire highly skilled techniques and a facility for such investigations. Operations research reports are informative, interpretive, and advisory in nature. They provide the research executive with objective data as a basis for administrative action.

Technical Feasibility Studies

Another aid to the executive administering the research organization is supplied by technical feasibility studies. These studies suggest new directions for research, new approaches that can be applied in existing programs, areas in which technical skills should be developed, and new techniques that should be explored. Technical feasibility studies provide data useful in evaluating technical programs and in formulating future plans.

Both operations research and technical feasibility studies provide objective recommendations with supporting background data. They are stimulants to dynamic operations. Whether established as formal staff functions operating in the office of the research executive or conducted less formally, operations research and technical feasibility studies are basic analytical techniques in the administrative process.

Capitalizing on Creativity

Industrial research is undertaken to capitalize on creative talent. It is a search for new knowledge resulting from a better understanding of phenomena, materials, and the arts. Productive research reflects an understanding of the research function and the ability to apply sound management principles in administering programs with the objective of capitalizing on creative talent. Effective research calls for channeling creative thinking into potentially useful and profitable directions. Research that does not pay off has no place in the corporate budget.

17

Fundamentals of Engineering Organization

TOPSY'S belief that she wasn't born but just "growed" aptly characterizes many engineering departments. Management concern is justified when engineers appear to be an aimless aggregate rather than a well-coordinated team.

Many weaknesses in the engineering program can be traced to organizational defects. Organization isn't a panacea for every problem in the engineering department, but a sound structure will carry the engineering manager over many rough spots that would spell disaster in an otherwise weak organization.

Sound structures provide a framework for effective engineering activities. Inadequate organizations magnify operating weaknesses. If engineering management knows what it wants to do and sets up the proper organization, staffs it adequately, and manages it soundly, any desired objective can be achieved—within practical limits. Success has been built on this principle. When the wisdom of this principle has been ignored, important engineering undertakings have failed.

The starting point in building a successful engineering operation is basic organization. Yet this vitally important first step is the last one taken by some engineering administrators.

Organization establishes the framework within which operations take place. Once the broad functions to be performed have been determined, the structure that is set up makes it possible to determine the interrelationships that should exist between these functions for maximum working effectiveness. In addition, formal organization steps put everyone concerned on notice that specific relationships do exist and are to be observed in the interests of harmony.

Organization is a continuing process. Not only must it precede operations but organization itself must develop along with engineering activities. Today's engineering operations can't be carried out effectively with yesterday's organization. Technology moves forward too rapidly for that. Technical organizations must keep pace by means of a continuous process of development. An organization begins to be outmoded by progress the moment the initial structure is completed. Organization development must be recognized as a continuing management function.

As rapidly as technological innovations appear, as promptly as engineering work points toward new horizons, the engineering organization should be revamped to fit new requirements. Acceptance of the need for such new requirements has been one of the secrets of success of expanding engineering departments in growth corporations.

The Administrator's Key Role

Sound management is based on successful practices. Fortunately, engineers can test ideas in the laboratory under carefully controlled conditions and on a scale commensurate with the risks and costs involved. On the unfortunate side, management ideas can rarely, if ever, be proved by a laboratory-scale experiment. Operations themselves must provide the proving ground.

Consequently, management knowledge must be gained largely from a study of the experiences of others. Because opportunities are limited for testing new concepts and ideas, it is even more imperative that these practices receive the careful attention and consideration of management lest new developments go unrecognized.

Final decisions on engineering management matters must be made by the engineering administrator. No one can execute the manager's function but the manager himself. His training, background, and experience represent years of preparation for decisions that he alone must make.

Execution of this responsibility calls for knowledge and facility in applying organizational concepts within the engineering operation. To a degree, outside assistance may be retained but the final responsibility for action rests with the engineering administrator. In any case, there are very few individuals who are competent to help him— demands on their time are heavy and their availability is limited.

Engineering administrators should be particularly critical in selecting outside consultants. They should inquire into the actual on-the-job
experience of the consultant in the particular field in which the consultant professes competence. Such references should be checked.

Anyone can call himself a consultant, yet few truly qualify. Those
who do are willing to provide references. References should include
those people who can testify as to the consultant's practical experience
on the job as well as those who can testify as to his ability to act
effectively in an advisory capacity.

The only type of individual whose consultation is worth much
to the engineering administrator is a man who, prior to undertaking
to offer a consulting service, has had from 10 to 20 years of experience
in industry in a responsible operating position in the area of his
subsequent professional specialty. The number of such individuals
available in relationship to the number who offer consulting services
is small.

It can be readily appreciated that the engineering manager's responsibility is not one that can be readily transferred even in part.
To act effectively, the engineering administrator should have a first-
hand appreciation of organizational fundamentals.

There isn't any best type of engineering organization. Every engineering group is faced with a different assignment. Individual assignments determine the type of organization needed for optimum output.

Objective organization planning is based on the jobs the engineering group must tackle. A model organization should be built around
actual requirements. The existing organization should then be compared with this model before any reorganization activity is
programmed.

Engineering managers experience most of their trouble in developing the model organization around basic work requirements. Once
this step is completed, once they have their model, it appears to
be relatively easy for them to reshape the existing structure to the
new pattern. The difficulty experienced in developing a model organizaton is usually traceable to the lack of a plan of attack. Armed
with a clearly defined course of action, engineering administrators
generally experience little difficulty in attacking organizational problems. Several clearly defined steps are recognizable as essential in
organization building.

Step 1: Define Functions to be Performed

Engineering objectives vary from company to company. Overall
objectives most commonly fall into eight categories.

1. Development of radically new products, processes, and manufacturing equipment
2. Development of lower cost products, processes, and manufacturing equipment
3. Development of new and improved functions in products, processes, and manufacturing equipment
4. Establishment of standards
5. Control of quality
6. Technical service to divisions and customers
7. Design and maintenance of production equipment
8. Technical counsel to corporation, cutomers, and special interest groups

In any engineering department, these broad objectives can be narrowed down into specific and immediate demands. Analysis of these specific demands on the engineering department will reveal to the engineering manager the types of distinct activities that must take place within the department.

These functions are either technical or administrative. These distinct activities are the building blocks of the organization. The failure to recognize each of these vitally important functions in developing an organization can result in seriously limiting the effectiveness of the organizational programming.

Step 2: Establish Functional Groupings

Technical considerations determine to a large degree the grouping of functions within the engineering department. Unfortunately, from an administrative position, this often results in an unwieldy structure. Not more than three individuals should report to the top engineering administrator if he is to have time to execute the responsibilities of his office. This policy must also be carried out at lower echelons. As managerial responsibilities give way to purely supervisory duties, the number of reporting individuals can be increased.

Experience has proved the engineering administrators are effectively served when engineering activities are reported to them through a technical director and an administrative director. There is considerable merit in this structure. Hard-to-find technical people are spared many time-consuming administrative duties. In addition, administrative duties are grouped with resulting uniformity of policies and procedures.

Whatever the decision with respect to reporting functions, in arranging groupings it is important to minimize the number of individuals reporting to those charged with managerial responsibilities. The allowable maximum appears to be three line executives reporting to the chief engineering executive. As many as five line managers may be acceptable in reporting relationships at lower echelons.

Step 3: Develop Line Relationships

The chief engineering executive occupies the top position in the line of authority for engineering activities. Centralization of authority in the hands of the chief executive provides for both flexibility and quick, decisive action. The premise is, of course, that he understands how to use his line executives in a way that permits them to operate efficiently.

Engineers in line positions should have complete authority to make all decisions on matters for which they are held responsible. Engineers who are placed in management positions without adequate authority to act lack one of the most important management tools. Engineers in line positions should be accountable to a single superior and in turn should establish simple and direct lines of authority and accountability within their own areas of responsibility.

Proper relationships between responsibility, authority, and accountability must be preserved if line organizations in the engineering department are to function smoothly. Each engineer in a line-management position is accountable only to the executive directly above him and he should be vested with complete authority associated with his area of responsibilities.

Step 4: Utilize Staff Services

Successful engineering administrators make use of staff services to multiply their effectiveness. Executives can't personally investigate every matter of importance related to their decision-making responsibilities. They can't stay informed on all subjects in rapidly advancing technological areas. No one has succeeded in being an expert in every field that the engineering manager must cope with in administrative work. Engineers who have tried have become so hopelessly enmeshed in detail that they have failed in their administrative assignment.

In these words from Plato's *Republic*, Socrates stresses the advantages of specilization: "Things will be better done when each man is free from the distraction of other occupations to do the job for which he is best fitted and to do it when it should be done." Astute engineering managers heed the wisdom of these words and capitalize on staff activities in distributing the details of their workload.

Staff functions relieve executive pressure in two principal ways: Portions of the executive's workload are absorbed, and requirements for specialized knowledge on the part of the executive are transferred to a staff advisory function. Staff members report directly to the executive. They are properly responsible for the specific investigatory, informational, and counseling services they provide to this executive. They are not responsible for any of the activities of the line executives in the next lower echelon, nor should they have any authority over them.

For example, a chief engineer may have three line executives who are responsible respectively for design, mechanical model development, and pilot production facilities. In addition to the three line executives responsible for these three departments, the chief engineer may have in his office a staff activity centered on operations analysis, one that periodically calls to the attention of the chief executive specific problem areas that are developing within the engineering departments. Recommended courses of action to alleviate this problem usually accompany such reports. The chief engineer may have another staff group reporting competitors' activities to him. Still other staff functions may appear.

All staff functions fall under one of these labels—investigatory function, information function, or counseling function. Each represents a segment of the engineering manager's responsibility, which has been detached and established as a specialized staff function in order to multiply the engineering manager's effectiveness.

Tests of Good Organization

Patterns for engineering organizations can't be picked out of the files. Engineering organizations must be tailored to the corporation's needs.

The ground rules for developing sound engineering organizations aren't as well developed as engineering managers might wish. Technological advances have taken place at such a rapid rate that a backlog of management experience has been difficult to accumulate. Organizations that have been developed according to known management fundamentals can be subjected to certain tests that will further show their inherent soundness. Eight tests have proved useful in this respect. From a structural viewpoint, engineering organizations that pass all eight tests are in a healthy condition.

1. Have areas of individual supervisory responsibility been clearly defined?
2. Has full authority been delegated to the engineer responsible for each activity?
3. Are engineering executives accountable to a single superior?
4. Is stability a characteristic of the organization?
5. Are individual functions balanced for harmonious working relationships?
6. Is the organization flexible?
7. Can the organization grow?
8. Is organization reduced to its simplest possible form?

Organizational simplicity is of such importance to overall soundness that it merits special consideration. Once an organization is completed, it should be subjected to one final test by applying this question to each position: Would the corporation suffer either the loss of immediate profits or long-range growth opportunities if this position were abolished?

Profits and Prospects

In today's competitive technological environment, the engineering organization's soundness determines to a large degree the corporation's future growth and progress. Farsighted management men are actively concentrating their attention on this phase of corporate activities.

The meagerness of the ground rules for organization development doesn't lessen in any way the vital importance of a sound engineering organization in the overall corporate framework. Some executives can be expected to be luckier than others in developing their engineering organizations. But for most the results will be directly related to the soundness of the approach to organizational development and the willingness to accept this task as a continuing, day-in-and-day-out executive responsibility. Happily, as a reward for a job well done, this assignment promises an increased and profitable output.

How to Organize Engineering for Product Development

The effectiveness of product development activities can be multiplied if management's first concern is focused on being certain that basic organizational functions are both present and operating. The burden of the workload in developing new products rests on research, engineering, and commercial development.

Every corporation carries on some product development work of a formal or informal nature. The problem confronting most companies is how to multiply its effectiveness. To accomplish this, both the staff and the organizaton must yield where necessary.

An attempt to increase output by effecting changes within the limits of existing organization patterns represents a halfway measure. The effective way is to establish requirements, determine organization fitted to the requirements, and then select from the present organization the personnel and facilities that fit the new patterns.

Ideas for new products are initially developed in many ways and through the efforts of many individuals, both from inside and outside the corporation. Once ideas have been established, the research, engineering, and commercial development departments digest these new ideas and, working with management, turn them into designs and specifications for profitable products.

These products must be more than just pieces of hardware. They must represent items carefully selected with a view to yielding a profitable return on the investment involved and so related to the overall activities of the corporation that the position of the corporation will be improved. While the activities of the research, engineering, and commercial development departments are closely interrelated, the respective functions involved are so distinct that each must be given separate attention.

Semantics introduce problems. The terminology for technical functions varies from corporation to corporation. This does not alter the nature of work performed but does confuse discussions of product development activities.

In the smaller company one man may be responsible for all product development activities, engineering, exploration of the commercial potential of new products, and any necessary research for product development. Larger corporations can assign one or more men to each of these activities. Regardless of staff size involved, the important point is that each of these functions plays an important part in developing a successful product.

Engineering Objectives

Engineering is responsible for creating and designing a product that can be produced economically and that will perform satisfactorily in the hands of the customer. For a product to do the job expected by the customer, it must incorporate design features that fill the requirements of distribution, installation, and adequate service maintenance throughout the product's life. The engineer assumes broad responsibilities. He must not only be creative but he must have the ability to turn his ideas into commercially feasible products. The engineer's job is to utilize existing knowledge in creating and designing products that can be produced and sold at a profit, and so he must concern himself with costs as well as technology.

Strengths and Weaknesses

There are relatively few really outstanding engineering organizations. Most engineering groups simply fail to meet the demands imposed by competitive industry conditions. Executives who are aware of this frequently experience difficulty in effecting remedial measures. Yet while there is a general lack of satisfaction with engineering efforts, there is no certainty about how to correct existing conditions.

In many companies, engineering management might be accused of being too busy to take time to adapt its operations to new conditions. The increasing importance of technology in modern industry calls for aggressive engineering leadership. In many cases, engineering management has not recognized this need.

The engineer's own outlook has, more often than not, limited full realization of his potential to the corporation. Initially the engineer's job was to solve problems presented by management. The technical group functioned to tell management what could not be done. Indeed, many of today's engineering organizations still limit their activities to this role.

To meet today's business needs, however, engineering must assume a more dynamic role. The first requirement is an objective, long-range planning of engineering programs. The second is aggressiveness combined with leadership and initiative. Engineering counsel must be injected into corporate affairs in broad areas encompassing research, production, marketing, sales, and finance—that is, if these functions are to operate at the level of effectiveness essential in a technological age. In long-established engineering organizations, bold and drastic management action will be necessary to develop a streamlined philosophy and a vigorous new outlook. Objective planning for engineering organization calls for an analysis of corporate needs, combined with a knowledge of engineering functions.

Basic Engineering Functions

Twelve major categories cover the functions of the engineering organization. Their relative importance will vary from corporation to corporation.

1. Management counsel on newly developing technology
2. Leadership in selecting areas for expansion of corporate activity
3. Creation of new products for management review
4. Design of commercially feasible products
5. Technical development of all product lines
6. Evaluation of proposed programs and projection of potential investment and expenses
7. Development of technical data covering physical plant equipment and process requirements
8. Maintenance of continuing quality control of operations and products
9. Acquisition of technical skills
10. Integration of technical information sources
11. Development of managerial talent for technical operations
12. Short- and long-range program planning in accordance with corporate objectives

Engineers who assume full professional responsibilities in this technological age are men who have the physical vigor and intellectual capacity to advance beyond the barriers that limit the man who must have a rule of thumb to guide every step he takes. The fulfillment of responsibilities imposed by basic engineering functions calls for qualifications that encompass administrative ability, technical knowledge and skills, creative ability, and a sense of perspective that provides a feel for the future.

Engineers meeting these qualifications do exist. Some have risen to become corporation presidents. Others are on their way up. But even more important, such talent is available in the lower echelons of engineering.

Some men are born leaders, but in most instances leadership is developed. The costly way to acquire engineering is to bid in the open market. The farsighted approach is through the creation of engineering organizations that develop engineering talent.

Dynamic or Static

No single structure is universally applicable. However, certain fundamental considerations can be established as guides. These considerations suggest action that can be taken to inject vitality into engineering organizations. In the final analysis, however, the proper course must be selected from existing alternatives. The final plan must apply these fundamentals in such a way as to optimize available skills, knowledge, experience, and innate capacity at both the administrative and the operating level.

Today's engineering role has become complex; rapid growth and change complicate the picture still further. Dynamic engineering organizations must replace static ones; patterns must be fluid rather than frozen.

To achieve this, four key functions are essential. These call for a separation of technical and administrative functions, and provide for continuing operations research and technical feasibility studies. The four key functions are represented by the administrative director,

Exhibit 6. Engineering department organization.

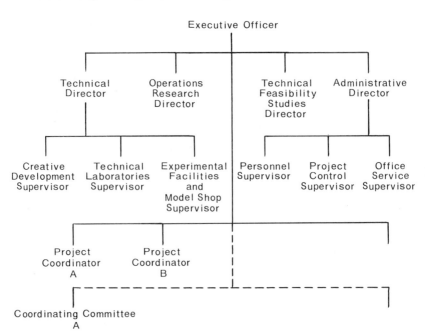

the technical director, the operations research director, and the technical-feasibility-studies director.

Interpretation of the key functions depends on the ability to discriminate between local (within the corporation or trade group) usage of specific terminology and the broader underlying concepts. The structural relationship of these four functions and other functions to be discussed are shown in Exhibit 6.

The Administrative Function

Engineers often voice the complaint that too much of their time is taken up with administrative work. In many cases the complaint is justified. Not only is this a source of annoyance to the engineers, but it means corporations are diverting valuable engineering talent to activities wasteful of both time and money. Separation of administrative and technical assignments is essential if engineering organizations are to be geared for efficiency and effectiveness.

The administrative director is responsible for business relationships in the engineering organization. His area of activity can be further divided into three general supervisory categories under his direction—planning, organizing, and controlling engineering department work.

The project control supervisor is responsible for schedules. New programs to be undertaken must be broken down into manpower and facilities requirements and then compared with available supplies of each resource. Based on this analysis, time schedules are established compatible with the men, money, and physical tools available for the project.

The advice of those who will execute the programs must be relied on for the information that goes into making up schedules. The supervisor should make no attempt to act as an expert in any area of technical specialization. Rather, it is his duty to search out counsel to establish reliable estimates.

Once programs are initiated, the project-control supervisor measures progress, with the help of the technical staff, against the original estimates. Deviations from schedules indicate the need for revision. Original and revised schedules reveal the degree to which objectives are being achieved in accordance with expectations.

The personnel supervisor is responsible for recruitment and placement of all personnel in the engineering organization and for professional development programs. Final selection of candidates for positions is made by individual supervisors and those designated by them to make this selection. Complete indoctrination of new members of the staff and all other personnel relationships in the engineering organization are the responsibility of the personnel supervisor.

The office service supervisor is responsible for providing secretarial staff, report-preparation facilities, library services, and related functions essential to the smooth working of the engineering organization.

The Technical Function

The technical director is responsible for the quality and quantity of the engineering department output. Engineering output is informational in nature and takes the form of designs, detailed drawings, data, instructions, and reports relating to products, processes, applications, and facilities of many types. The technical director is responsible for acquiring or developing the latest knowledge and skills and applying these to achieve optimum results at the earliest time commensurate with low costs. The technical function can be subdivided into creative development, technical laboratories, experimental facilities, and model development.

The creative development supervisor is responsible for all design and engineering development programs. Here, products, processes, and facilities take shape. Problems may arise that call for investigational and analytical work in the technical laboratories or the model shop by the experimental group. The results of such programs feed back to the creative development group for reference and incorporation in new design and development.

The technical laboratories supervisor is responsible for developing skills and facilities essential to engineering analysis. Continuing effort should be expended in a regular program with the objective of developing new and better technical tools. These skills and facilities enable engineering to reach new horizons as basic engineering data is developed.

The experimental facilities and model shop supervisor is responsible for the construction and operation of models by which to learn performance characteristics. Such information is an essential part of engineering design and development activities.

The Operations Research and Technical Feasibility Function

Short-range programs of the engineering department would not be noticeably impaired if these two functions were omitted, but long-range internal development, both operationally and technically, would suffer greatly. These functions serve to prod internal development. They are antidotes to stagnation.

Operations research is concerned with analyzing performance, and not only that of the products of the engineering organization, but the performance of the organization itself. Alternative courses of action are compared and analyzed and new procedures are established to optimize total effectiveness.

Technical feasibility studies provide parallel knowledge of new skills and potentially useful techniques and materials. This study is purely an exploratory function and is only indirectly related to scheduled programs. Technical feasibility studies start with the premise that current programs are relatively obsolete. Based on this assumption, new approaches to technical problems are needed, new products and processes should be explored, new techniques created, and new skills developed.

The technical-feasibility-studies group has the assignment of recommending specific courses of action to continually revitalize the technical phase of engineering operations. At the same time, the operations research group has the responsibility of making specific recommendations growing out of analyses of procedural and functional relationships.

Both operations research and technical feasibility studies provide recommendations for planning. Both serve to combat organizational and operational stagnation. If established as formal activities, these two functions have a better chance of surviving the insidious inroads of immediate problems—daily demands usually of the first order of inconsequence. If allowed to get out of control, daily demands can result in the ultimate deterioration of engineering effectiveness.

The Project Administration Function

The engineering project itself creates the necessity for an engineering organization. The role of the project must never be overshadowed by prima donnas in supporting roles. Engineering effectiveness is measured in terms of successfully completed projects. The critical phase of sound project administration is establishing adequate liaison and providing management guidance.

The project coordinator is responsible for managing the project and, with the cooperation of a coordinating committee, for establishing the liaison essential to successful execution of the project. The number of projects assigned to an individual project coordinator is determined by the magnitude of programs involved. In addition to project responsibilities, project coordinators may have other assignments. For example, they may have engineering assignments as technical specialists on other projects. Technical manpower is a scarce resource. Its application must be sufficiently flexible to permit optimum utilization.

When a project is initiated, the engineering executive assigns it to the coordinator best qualified to manage the particular type of project it represents. Administrative capacity is the primary qualification essential in selecting project coordinators. A secondary qualification is broad knowledge of the technical area of the project. A broad background is more important than a high degree of specialization.

The project coordinator first studies the problem area and background of events leading up to the initiation of the project, with a view to establishing a coordinating committee. This committee includes individuals with a direct interest in the project. The committee charts the course the project will follow and the project coordinator is responsible for keeping on this course.

Engineering analysis and design are responsibilities of the technical director. Staff members are assigned to the project by the technical director and his supervisors. Management control data is developed by the administrative director. The project coordinator is responsible for the overall program.

The engineering executive is responsible for the creation and design of products that will prove profitable to the corporation in both short- and long-run periods. The contribution of the engineering group is the information that enables manufacturing to produce, and distribution to sell, a product that will provide the ultimate customer with the performance he seeks.

The role of the engineering executive is an exacting one. He must combine technical proficiency, breadth of thinking, and perspective in outlook in dealing with both today's product and products contemplated for the days ahead.

This role is not for the mechanic, the recluse, or the timid man. The engineering executive must be an aggressive leader, and his leadership must reflect competence, courage, and cooperation if he is to command the respect of his management associates.

Looking Ahead

An expanding economy in a technological age places exacting demands on engineering organizations, and not all engineering groups have the strength to meet these demands. Dynamic engineering organizations that have the capacity to grow are expanding rapidly while stagnant engineering groups are spending their time explaining why advanced programs cannot be carried out. Top management should not be saddled with such resistance. Combatting negative attitudes is a serious drain on management energy.

Remedial action can be taken, but bold and drastic action will be required in many corporations. Successful remedial action is dependent on executive ability to tailor individual organizational patterns to corporate objectives.

18

Evaluating
Engineering Operations

PROFIT goals dictate periodic tests of engineering vitality. When vitality is low, performance falls off and growth stops. Physical examinations are a must, but management concern is usually prompted by trouble—trouble that could have been avoided by a policy of routine audits.

Patterns for engineering audits are relatively simple: (1) examination of the company's own engineering operations, (2) examination of the practices of others, (3) development of new programs based on the findings.

Operations evaluations can be wide of the mark when undertaken without a well-organized plan of attack. Specific areas to be covered should be established in advance. Operations analysis represents no small undertaking when worthwhile results are to be developed.

An organizational analysis may result merely in a panoramic picture of engineering activities, or it may represent a valuable and critical penetration. The latter is the only worthwhile analysis. Management's objective is to increase the value of engineering's contribution to corporation profits.

Twelve criteria will be found useful in making an engineering audit. These criteria focus attention on critical and sensitive aspects of the technical organization. Each will be discussed in some detail, beginning with an analysis of the role of engineering goals.

1. *Clearly stated goals should be established.* The starting point in analyzing any engineering organization—your own or another's—is a study of the organization's goals. Surprisingly enough, one of the most difficult jobs in organizational analysis is that of obtaining a statement of objectives. Too often there doesn't appear to be any general agreement on objectives within the engineering organization.

If you don't know what you're trying to do, it's hard to do the job successfully. Engineering organizations are like individuals in this respect. Effectiveness is impaired when clearly stated goals are not established.

Engineering goals are determined by overall corporation goals. This fact has often proved a serious stumbling block for the engineering administrator. If corporation goals haven't been established, engineering goals can't be developed. Overall corporation goals must come first.

Goals should be specific to be effective. It isn't enough to say that profits are the goal or that stability is an aim. Goals should be spelled out in detail.

Clearly stated goals should answer such questions as the following: What are we trying to achieve? In what time period? By what means? Where should this take place? At what cost? Why?

A statement of engineering goals doesn't remove the responsibility for creative thinking on the part of the engineering staff in any way whatever. Suggestions for amplifying and modifying these goals should flow in a steady stream from the engineering organization to management for review and action.

Goals give direction to engineering activities. Much of the criticism of technical activities is traceable directly to the absence of clearly stated goals. Once established, they provide a basis for planning by the engineering administrator as well as a basis for measuring performance. Only with such administrative tools can the engineering administrator fill his proper role within the corporation. Only by knowing what he must deliver can he set about the task of insuring adequate performance.

2. *Engineering functions should be balanced against goals.* Most commonly, organizations are thought of in terms of organization charts. By themselves organization charts don't tell very much. Accompanied by a statement of the goals to be achieved, the organization chart provides part of the raw working data for a critical evaluation of an engineering organization.

Three questions are pertinent in making this evaluation: (1) Are all of the functions essential to the achievement of the desired goals accounted for on the organization chart? (2) Are any unnecessary functions present? (3) Are the functions stated in terms that can be easily understood?

The achievement of engineering goals usually calls for specific types of activities, both technical and nontechnical. Individual goals can be broken down into functions essential to their achievement. These functions can be checked off against those appearing on the organization chart.

In this process confusion often arises when an attempt is made to consider available manpower at the same time. This is a procedural error. Functional analysis should take place quite independently of manpower studies. Functions essential to the achievement of goals should be established with complete objectivity.

At a later point in the overall organizational analysis, it may be found that one man must perform two or more functions. By contrast, a single function may require the services of a dozen or more men. These findings at the proper time will constitute a vital part of the overall analysis, but such findings injected at this point in the evaluation impair objectivity.

Organizations must be built around functions, not men. This is not to subordinate the importance of the individual. Effectively placed manpower is the basis of economic activity. Misplaced manpower is costly for the corporation and frustrating for the individual. The development of organization around activities essential to the achievement of objectives insures that positions will be created wherein men may work with the greatest opportunity for efforts rewarding to themselves and to the corporation.

3. *Engineering standards should be mutually agreed on by top management and the engineering group.* Basically the question is: How good a product is to be designed? In organizational analysis the engineering standards referred to are quality standards that will be reflected in the corporation's products. Top management and the engineering group must be in agreement.

At the outset one point may be bothersome. Why do engineering standards enter into considerations having to do with organizational analysis? The quality of the work to be performed determines the character of the engineering organization that must do the job. A high-quality product demands top-level engineering ability.

A corporation may manufacture a product that will sell over the counter in cut-rate stores and a similar product that will be sold to customers who put performance ahead of all other considerations. One must be designed for price, the other for performance. One engineering group must sacrifice performance for cost advantages; the other, cost for performance advantages.

Top management and engineering administrators do not always reach mutual agreement readily with respect to standards of engineering activities. One group usually wants engineering operations on a higher professional plane than does the other. Agreement results from fact-gathering, analysis, and decision. Once the decision is made it should be accepted and adhered to in all engineering operations until new facts can be produced to form an acceptable basis for altering the original decision.

A lack of mutual agreement on engineering standards by top management and the engineering group may be an underlying source of organizational problems. As such, it may be extremely difficult to detect. Sound practice calls for probing into this possibility at the outset of an organizational analysis. Hidden ramifications can then be brought into the open, where they no longer cloud evaluation of other organizational factors.

4. *Strong leadership should be available.* Strong leadership is a catalyzing force in any group activity. Effective leadership can double and triple the output. Leadership creates team spirit. Strong leadership consists of more than merely giving instructions to a group. It is relatively easy to find people who can tell others what to do, but individuals who can assume full responsibility for leadership are rare.

The true leader, first of all, has the ability to stimulate in others a real desire to exercise the highest possible level of effort. Today we hear so much about incentives that we sometimes forget that incentives are a poor and costly substitute for dynamic leadership.

Second, he knows how to present assignments in such a way that a man understands why his individual role on the particular assignment is important and why he must concentrate on that particular assignment. Behind every good engineer lies a reason why he wants to do a good job. One of the causes of poor performance lies in a failure to link the engineer's basic desires and interests to the job at hand. A good leader spots these weaknesses where they exist and concentrates on developing a harmonious relationship.

Finally, a good leader knows how to instruct and guide associates in the performance of specific tasks. Good leadership not only shows the junior engineer how to execute today's assignment, but how to do it in a way that prepares him for tomorrow's assignments and responsibilities.

These are leadership roles. Accepted and carried out, they multiply the effectiveness of the organization's manpower. Analysis should reveal the leaders, where they are, and the spots where leadership is lacking. It is not enough to be capable of doing a job; ability must be coupled to leadership for organizational or personal growth.

5. *Policies should govern operations.* Engineering management can profit greatly from a review of its policies. Policies are basic management tools. They improve performance and lighten management's job. Engineering managers who find themselves faced with the necessity of making repeated decisions on similar matters can save themselves time by formulating policies covering the subject areas in question.

For example, in many engineering organizations, technical society memberships must be approved by the engineering administrator. A policy—and the reasons for it—outlining the basis for approval of technical memberships to be paid by the company will eliminate repeated decisions and clarify a matter of importance to all engineers in the department.

A parallel case is that of trips to technical meetings. Quite commonly engineers are completely in the dark as to whether or not such attendance is favored. Individually they must approach their supervisor, who in turn may be required to discuss the matter one level and sometimes as many as two levels higher in the engineering group. All of this could be expedited by a clearly stated policy.

Two possible reasons may explain the absence of policies. First, engineering management may not have been educated up to the level of policy development. Second, engineering management may not be sufficiently in control of the situation to permit policy development. Either fact is quite revealing.

Engineering managers cannot operate effectively without policies to cover recurrent matters. Time is wasted in making separate decisions, and decisions themselves are seldom consistent. Lack of consistency gives rise to further problems for the engineering manager. If it were possible to select a single criterion to serve as a measure of the quality of an engineering organization, it would probably somehow be based on a measure of the adequacy of the policies established to govern the group's activities.

6. *Engineering tools should be available.* The increasing technological complexities of our present way of living are reflected by the elaborate nature of the tools required by today's engineers. Today's computer, which may rent for $50,000 a month, is a far cry from the days when a $5 slide rule was the backbone of advanced engineering calculations. Yet unless engineering management is prepared to furnish these new tools and to replace them with even more

advanced tools as rapidly as they became available, engineering output will suffer both in quality and quantity.

An evaluation of the engineering organization, if it is to be part of a process of continually strengthening its role, must give careful consideration to an analysis of available tools. Such an analysis must be based first on a study of both the current state of technology and the direction indicated by those who are working at its horizon. The analysis should serve to reveal the tools needed to equip a technical group to do work guaranteeing that the corporation will not be left behind its competitors. Available equipment can be compared with the results of this study.

New tools represent a great deal more than timesaving devices in the usual sense of the word. An advanced computer can carry out calculations in an hour that an engineer with a mechanical desk calculator might require 15 years to complete. And by the time he did complete such a task, the results would have been rendered meaningless by the inexorable march of technology.

New tools also represent new technologies. Developments such as the nuclear reactor have become basic tools. To carry out an assignment in the area of power generation, propulsion equipment, or other major segment of engineering activity, an engineering laboratory must have such a tool available.

Knowledge of these requirements enters into the organizational analysis because the tools themselves may be determining factors in final decisions with respect to organizational development. "Too little, too late" can be very costly to the corporation's industry position and profit picture.

7. *Resources must be organized for performance.* Reporting relationships in the engineering department reveal some of the reasons for its effectiveness or ineffectiveness, as the case may be.

Recently the author visited the office of an engineering manager. Our discussions were interrupted by a succession of telephone calls and by staff members who dropped into this man's office to get decisions on matters of apparent importance. Apologizing for these interruptions, the engineering manager said that his group depended on him for every decision. Perhaps one should have been impressed by how busy he was, but the more realistic reaction was one of dismay. This man was too busy to think. Not only was his own time tied up needlessly but his staff members were wasting valuable time in contacting him about every decision.

The reason for this steady stream of interruptions became apparent when this question was posed: "Have you delegated authority to these men so that they can act on these matters on their own initiative?" The answer was no. This man apparently didn't know how to find out which of his engineers were capable of assuming added responsibility.

An administrator—and this applies to the top engineering executive—can't work effectively if he has more than three men reporting to him. Moreover, this is to assume that these three are highly competent men who can assume full responsibility for their respective areas of operation.

Adequate authority must be delegated to those in subordinate positions. Authority must be commensurate with responsibilities if subordinates are to act effectively. Clearly established channels of accountability will serve as effective checks on performance. If the reporting relationships among the various engineering functions are effective, they are a good illustration of why competent engineering managers are never too busy to think.

8. *Functions must be adequately manned.* Regardless of difficulties encountered in the manpower market, the right man for the right job is essential to optimum performance. Any relaxation of efforts in this direction is at the expense of output.

It has been said that organizations are built around men. More realistically, organizations are built around functions, but there is no output until these functions are staffed with the right kind of manpower. The first thing is to define the jobs one wishes to accomplish, then determine the functions essential to these jobs, and finally, staff these functions.

Manpower programs not based on this logical step-by-step procedure are bound to develop serious organizational problems. The performance of the best available men will be totally ineffective unless positions are clearly tied to overall goals. Before putting the man in a troubleshooting position, check his function in relationship to other functions and departmental goals.

Manpower selection should consider two aspects of the applicant: his ability to do the immediate job required of him and his ability to grow. Growth potential may be the more important one in the long run.

Few engineering assignments have static characteristics. What we sometimes consider a static job generally is an assignment that calls for an engineer to take hold of a project and to grow with that project in a rapidly changing technological environment. It can be said with considerable assurance that any assignment static in nature is not an engineering assignment.

9. *Corporation interests must come before personal interests.* How often do you find men placing personal interests before company interests? This is a matter of real management concern because it represents a loss in time and money. Engineers who don't place company business first can't perform at their top level. You can't put forth your best efforts when you aren't 100 percent behind your job.

One of the reasons for poor performance in the engineering organization is directly attributable to the fact that some engineers regard their own personal interests as something quite foreign to those of the corporation. Engineers aren't entirely to blame; management has been guilty in a number of instances of adopting a standoffish attitude in dealing with its engineers—an attitude that is quite understandably reflected by the latter.

In making an organizational evaluation, you need to know the degree to which engineers place their personal interests ahead of the corporation's interests. But this isn't enough. You also need to know the reasons for this attitude of passive cooperation.

Some pertinent questions to ask in this connection in conducting an organizational analysis are: Have the engineers been taken into management's confidence? Have they been acquainted with corporation interests? Do they know the whys and wherefores? Do they know the importance of their individual roles as engineers? Have policies been such that engineering efforts have been recognized?

A great many engineering hours are wasted because engineers aren't wholly behind their jobs. Corporation time is spent on personal projects. These men are working part time for the corporation and part time for themselves. Such men are actually wasting their own time and don't realize it. Because of their indifference they are failing to establish a record for themselves in the organization.

Most of these men can be guided into paths of greater productivity by aligning their interests with those of their employer. This is a management responsibility. Acceptance of this responsibility is a measure of management's effectiveness. The alignment of individual interests with those of the corporation is a measure of organizational strength.

10. *Planning should precede action.* Planned action is effective action. Few will disagree. Yet a good plan represents more than a way of doing something. A plan is a definitely determined basis for action. It represents a practical approach to the job at hand. It anticipates and allows for a more-than-average number of obstacles.

Engineers are supposed to be extremely practical, yet this attitude isn't always carried over into the management phase of engineering operations. Planning isn't always rigorous. It doesn't always anticipate trouble. Planning activities should undergo continuing scrutiny in the course of an organizational analysis.

Particular attention should be directed to three aspects of any plan. Does the plan represent a sound course of action? Does it represent a complete program? Does it incorporate alternative courses of action to be followed in the event that initially planned courses are blocked?

This last phase seems to give engineers the greatest difficulty. In substance it amounts to advance trouble shooting. You visualize the plan set in motion. Next you apply your imagination to the process of anticipating everything that can possibly go wrong with the plan. Then you plan around each of these difficulties in advance of its possible occurrence.

The tactics and strategy are similar to those employed when the nation's President visits town. He may be scheduled to travel by car down the main street, but the side streets are kept open and so is a street parallel to the main street. Should trouble occur, bypass arteries are in standby readiness.

11. *Operating controls should be functioning.* To conserve its own time, engineering management should establish a system of controls that provide checkpoints in all engineering operations. One of the secrets of good management is the efficient use of controls as time-savers.

Management men need to know the current status of operations at all times if they are to plan and regulate activities. In the course of an organizational analysis, controls should be identified and evaluated. Where are they located? What do they tell management? When do they tell management? Whom, specifically, do they tell? This last question can be extremely important. Instances have been observed of control systems that functioned perfectly in every respect but one—the data was not directed to management and therefore no effective action could be taken!

The time to establish controls is when programs are developed. At this point, while programs are foremost in mind, management is in a position to stake out control points where they are needed.

One of the most obvious factors to be controlled is that of timing. Engineering programs should be broken down into divisions of activity whose end product is readily distinguishable. Estimated time of arrival figures should be established for these distinguishable end products.

Both times and divisional points are interrelated elements of timetables. Times don't mean anything unless there is a clear line of delineation in activity. For example, checkpoints have been established by engineering managers calling for completion of half of a literature search by a certain time. Such checkpoints are obviously impractical. There is no way of knowing when you are halfway through a literature search any more than there is of knowing when you are halfway through thinking up a new idea. You can estimate the time required for each of these, perhaps, but you can tell how much time was required only after you have completed the activity. Detailed jobs, such as the preparation of tracings, can be checked at midpoints because the nature of the task is such that it can be broken down into readily recognizable segments.

Checkpoints should encompass quantitative and qualitative factors as well as timetables. Management should learn the answers to such questions as "How much?" and "How good?" at frequent intervals as programs unfold. It should be emphasized that these questions should be injected only at points at which it is possible to get informative data.

Controls are a management tool. They multiply management's effectiveness. Much can be learned about an engineering manager's method of operation from an analysis of the controls he employs.

12. *Operations should be researched.* In the course of analyzing an engineering organization, an examination should be made of operations themselves. It is easy to commit the error of looking at organization charts, studying goals and other factors, and then jumping to the conclusion that these tell the whole story. Sometimes they do, but more often they don't.

The only way to learn about an organization is to study its day-to-day workings. A comparison of daily working relationships with the more theoretical aspect of planning will reveal the full impact of the latter on actual operations.

Our primary interest lies in learning about the management process that produces the results gained by organizing efforts. Operations themselves tell the real story. Often, actual operations are found to be at considerable variance with the manner in which engineering managers visualize them. Such a situation creates speculation as to whether or not current operations are more productive, proceeding as they are, than they would be proceeding in accordance with the planned program.

Operations should be researched to establish actual concurrent and sequential working relationships for comparison with planned programs. In addition, operations should be studied as a basis for establishing new operational concepts that can be developed and implemented in the interests of improved engineering activities.

Engineering operations should also be studied in the context of the corporation's activities and products. Changes in procedures and systems outside the engineering organization that could have a marked effect in raising its levels of performance should not be overlooked where a net benefit would accrue to the corporation.

The need for operations research arises because new problems arise out of everyday working relationships. Problems are created when programs are put into motion. Unrecognized, these may represent either lost opportunities or hidden costs. By means of operations research, operating relationships can be capitalized on or modified in the interests of overall engineering effectiveness.

Analyze and Revitalize

The end product of an evaluation should form the basis for specific management action taken to strengthen engineering activities. Evaluation should be both qualitative and quantitative. Results should guide management in revitalizing the engineering group.

The 12 criteria presented are fundamental to sound engineering management. Their effectiveness will depend in part on management's skill in applying them. Increased profits can be the reward. Management must combine analytical skill with courageous action to strengthen the engineering organization. The result will be new and lower cost products, processes, and services—the basis of increased corporation earnings in the years ahead.

part four
Staffing

19

The New Product Manager: Filter or Innovator?

IF the new product manager is to get the job done, he must have a complete understanding of what top management expects him to do, his authority must be compatible with his responsibilities, and he must know how his performance will be measured. These things must be spelled out in his position profile.

But surprising things are revealed during the development of job descriptions. For example, a job description for a new product manager disclosed that the individual who held the position could not fulfill his responsibilities because of a lack of authority. Every time he needed additional data to determine the direction he should take, he would be at the mercy of the marketing and technical information organizations because he would lack the funds for such studies. Although this manager of new products was charged with the responsibility for making specific recommendations to management, he could be effectively blocked if others were too busy to cooperate.

Why Write Position Profiles?

Preparation of position profiles clarifies management thinking about two important aspects of each function.

Duty definition. Competent and experienced men can do almost anything, but only when they know what is expected of them. Experienced men want to review position profiles before they even consider an assignment. They know only too well the problems that arise in situations where latitude of movement is too restricted to allow them to do the job that should be done.

And job titles rarely tell what's really involved. For example, a new product manager in one company may have an advisory and coordinating role; in another company, he may be the chief executive officer of an autonomous operating unit responsible for carrying a new product through to completion. Only the position profile can spell out the details of the job he is expected to do.

Performance bench marks. Realistic criteria for measuring performance can be created only by defining the duties to be performed. If the new product manager is expected to come up with ideas for new products, the position profile tells him so. On the other hand, if he's only required to develop ideas already appraised and selected by top management, he'll also learn this from the position profile. A position profile tells him where to concentrate his efforts, what management expects of him, and how his output will be measured and evaluated. But whether he generates the new ideas or just develops the ideas of others, the manager of new ventures always occupies a position that is the focus of attention—he is continually doing something that's a departure from what's been done before.

The manager of new ventures isn't part of the old pattern in most companies. Since it's a natural reaction to favor the familiar old faces and ways of doing things and to oppose the unfamiliar, the new product manager is often a subject for censure and resentment. But as industry matures, he is finding an increasingly friendly environment. The bench marks of the new product function are being established with enough flexibility to allow the specifics of the job to be defined.

The Position Profile

Position profiles should cover five basic areas: a general introduction to the position, a definition of principal duties and specific responsibilities, the extent to which the manager may act independently, the reporting relationships between the manager and his superior, and the specific criteria that will serve as a measure of job performance.

Function. A general description of the position and statement of its basic purposes should form the preface to a position profile. This will serve to orient the reader to the nature of the position that is to be described in detail.

For the new product manager, responsible as he is for the company's new ventures, the function might be described as follows:

> Under the direction of _____ and within the framework of established company policy, the new product manager is responsible for the successful development and initial operation of new ventures in terms of achieving profit objectives in accordance with approved plans.

This general description of a function merely serves to set the stage for what is to follow—it recaps the essence of the job definition. In no way should this opening statement be at variance with any detail of the position description it precedes.

Duties and responsibilities. Simply stated, this part of a position description tells the project manager what is wanted in terms of action to be taken and responsibilities to be accepted.

In managing any new venture—from thinking about directions the company might take in the future to the development of profitable business in established areas—there are many specific duties and responsibilities that must be fulfilled. The new product manager should know which ones he must execute himself and which are the responsibilities of others in the company.

It should be recognized that if enough people in the company could take enough time away from their respective responsibilities to become familiar with the requirements of each new venture, all the functions essential to the success of new undertakings could be found within the going business operation. Because the required time isn't available when men are busy with their present jobs, the new product manager must duplicate some existing jobs in the interest of expediting a new venture. However, he and others should know in advance which functions are to be duplicated in the best interests of the project and the overall business of the company.

Even though this problem arises in other operating areas to some degree, nowhere is it as critical as in the matter of dealing with new ventures. In fact, the manager of new products must sometimes conduct the new venture as a small business within a larger business and duplicate almost every function in the company.

Because the items to be purchased are so different from those the purchasing department is experienced in buying and because the dollar volume is so small, the new product manager may be authorized to act as his own purchasing agent. He may hire his own people because the personnel department has set no criteria for the specialists he needs. He may set up his own research, engineering, and pilot production groups, again because the requirements of a new venture may be so different from what's been done before.

It is because of these unique requirements of the position that it is so important to define the makeup of the job to be done to put the company where it wants to be in the days ahead. A job description that adequately defines the new product manager's duties must outline all areas of his responsibility.

For example, the new product manager's responsibilities are frequently defined as responsibilities that include—

    Searching out new venture opportunities
    Determining criteria for selecting new ventures
    Making certain the right project is selected
    Developing project targets, timetables, and techniques
    Financial management of new product projects
    Determining functions to be staffed and determining which are
        to be executed by other departments
    Establishing customer specifications for end products of the new
        venture
    Basic research
    Prototype development
    Preliminary market studies
    Production of pilot quantities
    Pioneer sales
    Procurement of sales required to develop the new venture
    Development of distribution channels for the new product
    Future planning—beyond the immediate needs of planned new
        ventures
    Terminating unprofitable projects

It is not necessary or, in many cases, desirable for a new product manager's responsibilities to embrace every item in the foregoing list. However, it is necessary for him to know that his duties can range from full responsibility for the management of an autonomously organized project operation to the coordination of project work parceled out to other departments of a going business operation.

Authority. Once the duties and responsibilities of a new product manager have been defined, the areas in which authority to act must be granted are clearly established. To effectively carry out specific objectives, the new product manager must be given full authority to make final decisions in the areas that control the objectives.

If he must request approval each time he wants to take specific action, responsibility is, in effect, shifted to the person who grants approval. If he is turned down when he makes a request, the fate of the project is automatically placed in someone else's hands.

Adequate authority can be spelled out in such a simple way as this: "The manager of new product ventures has the authority to act within the limits of the budget for his operations, which he has prepared and which has been approved by management. All actions are to conform to the company's standard operating policies."

Notwithstanding the direct tie between authority and responsibility, considerable confusion still exists in the minds of many managers. If facts are faced rationally, it cannot be disputed that the man who makes decisions is the man with whom responsibility rests for the success or failure of any undertaking. Responsibility and authority cannot be separated.

Those who assist decision makers are only advisers and act only in an advisory capacity, and their duties and responsibilities should be defined as advisory. The man who makes the final decision decides whether or not to use the advice he is given.

Reporting relationships. The manager of new ventures should report to men who can grant the kind and scope of authority needed to manage projects effectively. Executives cannot grant authority that exceeds the authority they themselves hold. For example, if a vice-president in charge of a division of a multidivision company is authorized to approve capital expenditures up to $100,000, he must limit a project manager who reports to him to something less than $100,000 of capital expenditures.

Since the manager of new product ventures is limited in his authority by the authority of the man to whom he reports, he should report high enough in the organization structure to act effectively. Financial considerations aren't the controlling factor. Most important are considerations relating to the different kinds of business activity the company would consider entering. Such decisions are generally made by the board chairman, president, or executive committee. In divisionalized company operations, such decisions may be made by the divisional vice-president or general manager. But in any case, the manager of new products should report at levels where final decisions about new ventures are made.

Standards of performance. Some more or less well-defined criteria are applied to everyone's work. A production worker's performance, for example, may be measured in terms of output and quality, but measurement criteria differ with the kind of work. While productivity and costs may be suitable partial measures of a production manager's output, criteria such as sales volume and industry position must be applied to the sales manager's work. In each case, criteria used to measure individual performance should be suited to the kind of performance that will most benefit the company.

The manager of new ventures is no exception to the rule. Someone in the company must pass judgment on this man's work and say whether he has done a good, mediocre, or poor job. Furthermore, performance evauation will probably be made against specific point-by-point accomplishment criteria. Judging a man's work after a job has been done is always important, but unless the standards of performance used as a basis for this judgment are made known in advance, the greater part of their effectiveness is lost. The new product manager needs to know how he's to be judged, and these performance standards are valuable checkpoints. He may be able to measure his progress by answering several very pertinent questions:

Are phases of new ventures completed according to plan?

Has any deviation from plan been justified by developments that could not be anticipated but that were detected through diligence and skill before unnecessary time and money had been expended?

Are phases of new ventures soundly organized to maintain anticipated return on investment, profit level, and payout position?

Have present programs and anticipated future requirements been updated?

It's impractical to establish performance standards for the manager of new ventures that do not involve the exercise of considerable judgment. But at the same time, it is a serious error for someone with this management responsibility to think that his performance is not to be under critical review at all times. Any experienced new product manager knows that standards will be used in evaluating his effectiveness, and he will want to know what they are in advance.

Hindsight is always easier to apply than foresight. The Monday morning quarterback always knows how the game could have been won. Yet it isn't of much comfort to a man, or to a company, to know how a project should have been managed after it's too late to do anything about it.

The time for management to do its homework is before the job starts—by defining the makeup of the job to be done. This is the function of the position profile.

20

Developing
Creative Capabilities

CREATIVE thinking is a scarce commodity, perhaps because creative thinkers have traditionally been the product of a spontaneous process. The shortage of such thinkers will continue as long as the supply depends on self-stimulation.

To increase the output of new ideas, management must focus its efforts in the direction of stimulating an accelerated flow of ideas. The creative process is susceptible to such stimulation.

Studies of this process by competent analysts reveal that while some people may be more creative than others, everyone has creative ability. However, only a relatively few individuals seem to know how to tap their creative potential. Fortunately, studies have revealed some vitally important aspects of the creative process, and while it is recognized that there is a great deal more to learn, tangible results can be achieved by putting to work what is already known.

Barriers to Creative Thinking

The first step in developing creative thought processes is one of clearing the tracks of all obstacles. The barriers to creative thinking fall into three groups—analytical, social, and emotional. Classified under these headings, recognized barriers to creative thinking are as follows.

Analytical Barriers
Failure to recognize the problem
Failure to recognize all environmental factors
Inclusion of extraneous environmental factors
Failure to observe all factors
Failure to associate cause and effect

Social Barriers
Conformity
Cooperativeness
Competitiveness

Emotional Barriers
Unwillingness to dream
Desire to be logical
Fear of ridicule
Desire for security
Superficiality
Wishful thinking
Surrender to novelty
Resistance to change
Distrust of others
Lack of reward stimulus

These three groups of factors exert their influence in somewhat differing ways.

First of all, one's power of analysis, or his perceptiveness, will determine his ability to visualize new concepts clearly and recognize them as such. Most of us, on occasion, recognize certain innovations as ideas we have already entertained. We rationalize the situation by telling ourselves that we were too busy with other more important matters to take time to act when the idea first occurred to us. Undoubtedly this is partly true, but whether we wish to accept it or not the real truth of the matter is often traceable directly to the fact that we didn't recognize the full implications of the idea. Our creative ability was blocked by our inability to properly analyze the situation.

We have considered here a situation wherein we had an already formulated and recognizable concept. Many ideas remain unformulated and therefore unrecognized because of impairments in our analytical ability. The creative process is blocked because data vitally important to the process was not collected, because extraneous factors were introduced, and because proper relationships in the working data were not established. These ideas never come to the surface.

Equally important is the social barrier. Conformity, cooperativeness, and competitiveness have a deadening effect on creative tendencies. The conformist, by definition, adheres closely to convention. Such an attitude rarely stimulates a flow of new ideas. In a like manner, the cooperative individual is more likely to acquiesce than to strike out for something new and novel.

The competitive attitude might be thought to favor innovation, but competitive tendencies actually limit the individual insofar as innovation is concerned. The competitive individual has a goal he wants to achieve, and in striving to reach it, he thinks he runs the least risk by adhering to the course of action being followed by those with whom he is competing. In this respect he relegates competition to a matter of degree of effort. He may not wish to acknowledge the fact, but he is more certain of his untapped energy than of his untapped creative ability.

Social attitudes limit the thought process by channeling it in preestablished patterns. Emotional responses, to consider the third barrier, take on a great many different forms. For example, someone who has been brought up to believe that daydreaming is a waste of time won't produce many new ideas until he overcomes that belief. New ideas can take shape only when the thinking process is allowed to run wild.

A logical course of reasoning will reject concepts that don't fit into this pattern of thought. The formal logic behind many good ideas has been developed to defend itself against the embarrassment of a demonstrated fact. Fear of ridicule, desire for security, and many other emotional responses similarly limit creative thinking.

No one can ever free himself entirely of all the barriers to creative thinking. But recognition of their existence serves as a reminder to check constantly for their presence. A knowledge of the nature of these barriers permits continuing self-analysis and mental housecleaning, thereby clearing the way for creative thought.

The Creative Background

Creative work has flourished in the presence of specific background factors. Some factors stimulate creative work; others accelerate creative thinking once the process is started. Six factors have been found important in creating a background for creative work:

1. Personal acceptance of inherent creative ability
2. Broad training and experience

3. A questioning approach
4. Acute powers of observation
5. Capacity for concentration
6. Ability to associate ideas and facts in new relationships

One of the essential ingredients of an atmosphere for creative work is the individual's personal conviction that he has the capacity for it. This must be accepted from the outset, for it is extremely difficult, if not impossible, to do creative work if one takes a negative attitude with regard to his creative ability.

Broad training and experience provide both a reference structure of factual knowledge and known working relationships. This greatly facilitates the thinking process. It eliminates time that would otherwise be lost in reestablishing known facts. The absence of broad training and experience generally slows down the creative process, sometimes to a standstill.

A questioning approach is the door-opener in the creative process—it reveals gaps and uncertainties. The greatest catalyst in the creative process is the question "Why?" and a close runner-up is the question "Why not?" Both questions stimulate creative development. Ask them, and you find yourself in the midst of creative activity.

Acute powers of observation supply the working material for creative activity. This is the fact-gathering and fact-verifying mechanism in the creative process. To aid the creative process, powers of observation must be active, accurate, and capable of scanning a wide field.

The questioning mind must be capable of quickly visualizing the environment surrounding the problem. Then it must have the ability to concentrate at will on a single problem of its own selection. The ability to devote full attention to one subject for long periods of time has been held to be absolutely essential for any markedly creative efforts.

In the course of this concerted effort the individual's ability to associate facts and ideas in new relationships will come into play. Those who have a highly developed facility for reconstructing material in the form of new models will be most efficient in quickly reviewing a large number of potential relationships.

A Plan for Creative Action

No known formula exists to direct creative thought, but an individual plan of action can be developed to put the parts of the process in a sequence that has proved helpful. Eight steps are required. At any point in the process it may be necessary to stop and start the process over again. This does not suggest that an error has been made but rather that new knowledge has been developed necessitating a revision or expansion of earlier groundwork.

By no conceivable stretch of the imagination can it be anticipated that creative thinking will result from any specific course of action. All that can be said is that creative thinking is more likely to result from a carefully engineered approach. On this premise, careful consideration should be given the role of each of the following.

1. *Establish the problem area.* The most productive thought process results from efforts centered on a particular problem. Delineation of the problem establishes the area on which attention should be focused. This step should not restrict thinking, but rather spotlight every aspect of the problem on which attention should be concentrated.

2. *Collect pertinent facts and ideas.* Once a problem area has been selected and defined, it is helpful to collect as much information as possible relating to the problem. Factual data and ideas are both important at this stage. Their ready availability for quick reference minimizes interruption in the thought process. Interruptions in creative thinking can be costly. Factual data is essential reference material. Ideas can be equally important. A knowledge of already existing ideas serves both reference purposes and helps suggest new concepts and relationships.

3. *Construct existing relationships in the problem area.* Facts are of primary importance when their relationships to each other are established. Bits of knowledge become usable when we establish relationships between two or more pieces of data. Ideas are mental mosaics. They are visualizations of useful relationships. A construction of existing relationships puts facts and existing ideas in their most readily available form for reference purposes.

4. *Develop possible new relationships.* Taking what is known and developing new concepts is sometimes considered the only important step in the creative process. It will become immediately apparent that this is not true if we look back to each of the preceding steps, all of which have called for a degree of active creative thinking. Positioning the problem in relation to its environment, screening the problem area, selection of factors and orientation are all part of the creative process. If recognition is not given each of these, the mental process is slowed down. Ultimately, creative powers may be shut down.

Developing possible new relationships is a step in applying conscious effort to reassemble facts and ideas into new associations. How many different ways can they be associated? What is the practical significance of each of these different models? How can they be modified to develop still other relationships? These questions suggest aspects worthy of exploration.

5. *Incubate.* There comes a time to get away from the subject, to stop application of conscious effort and to forget the whole thing. Let the subconscious mind go to work while turning conscious thought to other matters. Meanwhile, note any new ideas.

6. *Synthesize optimum relationships.* After a time period that will vary with the individual, conscious effort again comes into play. Returning to the problem area, you should review all new ideas and screen them to select the best combination of variables. Earlier probing has probably involved separate treatment of a variety of important facets of the problem. Ultimately these should be fitted together and examined as a whole.

7. *Evaluate.* A critical look at the idea from a very practical viewpoint is next in order. Up to this point the mind has looked at combinations and permutations of data. Now it asks such questions as: Is it usable? Is it acceptable? How does it fit into the present scheme of things?

8. *Develop dynamic concepts.* Creative action in the final phase should reshape ideas into vividly portrayed concepts that can be readily interpreted by others. Effective creative thinking must develop ideas that can be communicated to someone else.

In the absence of a specific plan of action, the creative thinking in the solution of a problem can be expected to vary widely. The best thing to do is to approach problems in the way that has produced the best yield of new ideas.

Injecting Creativity into Daily Activities

Individual progress is dependent to a very large degree on the ability to inject creativity into daily activities. Yet very little effort is applied to the development of creative ability—an expenditure that holds the promise of sizable returns.

A profitable starting point for any activity lies in the development of creative ability. This can be accomplished by (1) removing the barriers to creative thinking, (2) establishing a background for creative thinking, and (3) approaching problems in a manner designed to bring creative powers into play. All of this amounts to engineering the creative process.

Index

administrative director, engineering, 185
administrative function, engineering, 185–186
administrator, engineering, 175–176
alternatives in decision making, 126
application, new products, 119
applied research supervisor, 169
assumptions and new product failures, 108–109
authority, new product manager, 206–207

basic research supervisor, 169
Bulova Watch Co., 136, 142
business, defining nature of, 142–143
buying decisions and price, 44–45
byproduct benefits in decision making, 128

capabilities, defining, 141–142
capital
    cost of, in product development, 54–56
    present value of future outlays, 55
Carlson, Chester, 138

cash flow, discounted, 55, 57, 61
change, adapting to, 149
Cincinnati Milacron Co., 142
commercial development group
    definition of commercial potential, 153–156
    detection of ideas and markets, 153
    organization of, 158–160
    role of, 151
commercialization, new products, 120–121
commercial opportunities, definition of, 153–156
competition
    with customers' sales, and new product failures, 110–111
    defining, 143–144
    for new products, 39–40
    and product development, 19–20
    research activity of, 163–164
competitive conditions and new product failures, 113–114
consultants, use in troubleshooting and problem solving, 11
controls, engineering, 198–199
corporation interests
    and acceptability of ideas, 35–36

corporation interests (*continued*)
  and new products, 25–26
  vs. personal interests, 197
cost
  of capital in product develop-
    ment, 54–56
  commitment of, in decision mak-
    ing, 128
  competitive opportunities in,
    94–95
  lower, and new product, 24–25
  monitoring, 130–131
  new products, 40
  and pricing of new products, 50
  product development, 53–54,
    66–68
  vs. profits, 9–10
  of research results use, 164
creative development supervisor, en-
    gineering, 186
creativity
  action plan, 212–214
  background for, 211–212
  barriers to, 209–211
  capitalizing on, 172–173
  in new product panel, 28
customers' changing needs and new
    product failures, 107–108

decision making
  agreement in, 129
  alternatives in, 126
  cost commitment in, 128
  dilemma in, 148
  on product development pro-
    grams, 156–157
  profile, 125–126
  reappraisal points, 128
development cost, new product,
    53–54
development time, new product, 53
discontinuities
  technological, 136–137
  utilization, 137–139
discounted cash flow, 55, 57, 61

distribution
  new products, 39, 122–123
  profit opportunities in, 76–77
Dow Chemical Co., 140
downgrading and new products, 25
Du Pont, E. I. de Nemours & Co.,
    Inc., 140

earnings and size, growth in, 8–11
Eastman Kodak Co., 137
economic analysis supervisor, com-
    mercial development, 158–159
employees, contractual agreements
    on trade secrets, 88–89
engineering
  administrative function, 185–186
  administrator's role, 175–176
  controls, 198–199
  corporation vs. personal interests,
    197
  dynamic vs. static, 184–185
  evaluation criteria, 190–200
  functional groupings, 177–178
  functions, 176–177, 183
  goals vs. functions, 191–192
  leadership, 193–194
  line relationships, 178
  manning, 196
  objectives, 181–182
  operations research and technical
    feasibility function, 186–187
  planning and action, 197–198
  policies and operations, 194
  and product development,
    180–181
  profits and prospects, 180
  project administration function,
    187–188
  resources and performance,
    195–196
  staff services, 178–179
  standards, management agree-
    ment on, 192–193
  strengths and weaknesses, 182
  technical function, 186

engineering (*continued*)
    tests of good organization,
        179–180
    tools, availability of, 194–195
engineering executive, 188
evaluation
    new products, 42, 118–119
    product- vs. market-oriented,
        151–152
experimental facilities and model
    shop supervisor, engineering,
        186

feasibility studies, technical, 172,
    187
forecasting, technological, oppor-
    tunities highlighted by, 140–141

General Electric Co., 140, 141
General Tire and Rubber Co., 142,
    143
Gillette Co., 143
goals
    definition of, and new product
        failures, 109–110
    vs. functions, engineering,
        191–192
    engineering organization, 191
Goodyear Tire & Rubber Co., 143
growth
    ingredients, 2
    profit vs. sales, 62
    size vs. earnings, 8–11

Honeywell Corp., 141

ideas
    appraising, 34–35
    catalyzing flow of, 29–30
    clarification of, 154
    detection of, 153
    development of, 31
    new product panel in generating,
        27–28
    sources of, 28–29
    tapping source of, 30–31

ideas (*continued*)
    and trade secrets, 86
    unacceptable, 35–36
income analysis
    by product line, 99
    in product program, 97–98
industry position and product devel-
    opment, 61
information and trade secrets, 86
installation, profit opportunities in,
    79
International Business Machines
    Corp., 137–138
investment
    vs. profit, 52–53
    research, 164

know-how and trade secrets, 84–85

laboratory supervisor, research, 169
licenses and new products, 38
Linde Air Products Co., 141, 142
line relationships, engineering, 178
literature study, new products, 41–42
loss leaders vs. profit leaders, 10–11

maintenance, product opportunities
    in, 80–81
management
    and engineering standards,
        192–193
    and idea development, 31
    and product development pro-
        grams, 154
manning, engineering, 196
manufacturing, profit opportunities
    in, 73
market(s)
    competitive opportunities in, 95
    detection of, 153
    new product, 24
    and technology, integrating,
        150–160
market analysis supervisor, commer-
    cial development, 159

market appraisals for new products, 38–39
market measurement and new product failures, 112–113
Minnesota Mining and Manufacturing Co., 141, 143
mousetrap fallacy, 33–34

nearest equivalent product (NEP) and new product pricing, 47–48
needs vs. wants in product design, 33–34
newness, nature of, 23–25
new product(s)
    appraisal and evaluation, 42, 118–119
    appraising ideas, 34–35
    characteristics of, 23–25
    checkpoints, 117–123
    choice of, 52–62
    competition for, 39–40
    competitive opportunities in introductory phase, 94–95
    decision and action, 42–43
    failure, reasons for, 104–116
    literature study, 41–42
    manager's function, 204–205
    markets, 24
    obsolescence, technological, 40–41
    pricing, 44–50
    profitability projections, 51–62
    technical–economic analysis, 36–41
    see also product development
new product manager, position profile, 204–208
new product panel, 26–27
    in generating ideas, 27–28

objectives
    agreement in validating and modifying, 130
    commercial development group, 152–157
    engineering, 181–182
    by phases, 127–128

objectives (*continued*)
    product development, 75–76
    research, 162
    statement of, 127
office services supervisor
    engineering, 186
    research, 168
operations research, 171–172
    engineering, 186–187
    see also research
opportunities
    failure to recognize, and new product failures, 111
    highlighted by technological forecasting, 140–141
    in industry posture, 147–148
organization
    commercial development group, 158–160
    engineering, 174–189
    research programs, 165–173

packaging, profit opportunities in, 75–76
patentability and product development, 155
patents
    and new products, 38
    vs. trade secrets, 88
payback, product development, 56–57, 61
performance
    and competitive opportunities, 95
    measurement areas, 3–7
    new products, 24
    position profile bench marks, 204
    standards, new product manager, 207–208
personnel, performance measurement, 6
personnel supervisor
    engineering, 185–186
    research, 167–168
planning
    and action, engineering, 197–198
    performance measurement, 6

planning (*continued*)
  and product development, 18–19,
    68–69
plant tours and trade secrets, 89
policies, performance measurement,
  6
position, performance measurement,
  5
position profile
  need for, 203–204
  new product manager, 204–208
practicality and new product fail-
    ures, 106–107
present products
  action areas, 73–81
  as profit base, 72–73
  profit potential, 81
present value
  dollar, 58–60
  of future outlays, 55
  of future returns, 57
price
  and buying decisions, 44–45
  and sales volume, 46
pricing
  competitive products, 45
  new product vs. nearest equiva-
    lent product, 47–48
  profit opportunities in, 77–78
  specialty products, 45
  strategy, 46–47
pricing profile, 48–49
problem solving, responsibility for,
  11
processes and trade secrets, 85–86
product(s)
  addition vs. deletion, 9
  performance measurement, 5
  utilizing potential of, 144
  see also new products; present
    products; product develop-
    ment; product life cycle
product analysis supervisor, com-
    mercial development, 159
product concept, 35
  fallacious, 33–34

product design, needs vs. wants in,
  33–34
product development
  breaking away from the past in,
    20
  and competition, 19–20
  cost, 53–54, 66–68
  cost of capital in, 54–56
  engineering and, 180–181
  experience in, 17–18
  facilities for, 21
  funding, 65–71
  and industry position, 61
  knowledge and ability in, 16–17
  objectives, 67
  payback, 56–57, 61
  perspective in, 19
  phases, 118–123
  planning and, 18–19, 68–69
  protecting ideas in, 20–21
  questions on, 21–22
  steps in, 16
  success record, 62
  time for, 15–16
  see also new products; present
    products; product life cycle
product development programs
  decision making on, 156–157
  direction of, 157
  technical–economic factors,
    155–156
production, new products, 121–122
productivity
  performance measurement, 4
  research, 164
product life cycle
  competitive phase, 93
  developmental phase, 97
  dropout phase, 94
  growth phase, 95
  introductory phase, 94–95
  obsolescent phase, 93–94
  potentially profitable phase, 96
  prospective phase, 96
  scheduled phase, 97
  speculative phase, 96

product line
  balancing, 92–93
  component standardization, 74–75
  income analysis by, 99
  incompatibility with, and new
    product failures, 114–115
  simplification, 74
product plan, risk in, 8
product portfolio analysis, 98–102
product programs
  auditing, 91–103
  case study, 97–102
  synchronizing efforts, 93–96
product proposals, overselling, and
    new product failures, 114
profit(s)
  vs. costs, 9–10
  and engineering organization, 180
  growth rate, 62
  vs. investment, 52–53
  new products, 40
  or pitfalls in fads and fashions,
    145–147
  from research, 162–163
profitability
  new products, 51–62
  performance measurement, 3–4
profit leaders vs. loss leaders, 10–11
profit opportunities in present prod-
    ucts, 72–81
progress, performance measurement,
    7
project administration function, en-
    gineering, 187–188
project control supervisor
  engineering, 185
  research, 167
project coordinator, engineering,
    187–188
project supervisor, commercial de-
    velopment, 158
proprietary position, *see* trade
    secrets

reappraisal points
  agreement in scheduling, 130

reappraisal points (*continued*)
  in decision making, 128
reporting relationships, new product
    manager, 207
research
  administrative function,
    167–168
  engineering operations, 199–200
  executive and his role, 170–171
  investment, 164
  objectives, 162
  organization for, 165–173
  productivity, 164
  profitable projects, 165
  profits from, 162–163
  scientific function, 168–169
  spending for, 163–164
resources and objectives in decision
    making, 127
responsibilities
  new product manager, 205–206
  profit producing, 2–3
  research executive, 170–171
  for trade secrets, 83
restyling
  competitive opportunities in, 95
  and new products, 25
review points
  agreement in scheduling, 130
  in decision making, 128
risk in product plan, 8

sales
  customers', and new product fail-
    ures, 110–111
  growth rate, and product develop-
    ment, 62
  gross, and product development,
    61–62
  volume, and price changes, 46
selling, profit opportunities in,
    78–79
servicing, product opportunities in,
    80–81
size and earnings, growth in, 8–11

staff director, commercial development, 159
staff services for engineering organization, 178–179
staff supervisors, commercial development, 158
success, probability of, in decision making, 128
supervisor
    applied research, 169
    basic research, 169
    commercial development projects, 158
    commercial development staff, 158
    creative development, engineering, 186
    economic analysis, commercial development group, 158–159
    engineering office services, 186
    engineering personnel, 185–186
    engineering project control, 185
    engineering technical laboratories, 186
    experimental facilities and model shop, engineering, 186
    market analysis, commercial development, 159
    product analysis, commercial development, 159
    research laboratory, 169
    research office services, 168
    research personnel, 167–168
    research project control, 167
supply and demand disparity and new product failures, 115–116

tactics, targets, and timetables, 127–129
technical director, engineering, 186
technical–economic analysis, new products, 36–41

technical–economic factors in product development programs, 155–156
technical feasibility studies
    engineering, 187
    research, 172
technical laboratories supervisor, engineering, 186
technical programming, payoff in, 146–147
technological development as threat to new products, 40–41
technological forecasting, opportunities highlighted by, 140–141
technology
    and markets, integrating, 150–160
    strategic attack on new, 139–140
    tapping cross talk, 144–145
time factors, monitoring, 130–131
timetables, targets, tactics, and, 127–129
timing, in new product failures, 105–106
trade secrets
    employee contractual agreements, 88–89
    giveaway of, 89–90
    makeup of, 84–86
    vs. patents, 88
    protection of, 82–83, 90
    recognition of, 84
    responsibility for, 83
    tests of, 86–87
    theft of, 82
    unsolicited disclosure, 90
troubleshooting and problem solving, consultants in, 11

Union Carbide Corp., 141, 143
upgrading and new products, 25
utilization, product opportunities in, 79–80

12/17/88